THE GENESIS OF FORM

MARK VERSTOCKT

THE GENESIS
OF FORM

FROM CHAOS TO GEOMETRY

MULLER, BLOND & WHITE

Frontispiece PAUL KLEE, *Pastorale* 1927. Tempera on canvas (69.3 × 52.4 cm).
Collection The Museum of Modern Art, New York.
Abby Aldrich Rockefeller Fund and Exchange.

First published in Holland in 1982 by
Verantwoordelijke Uitgever: Scriptoria n.v.,
Belgielei 147a Antwerp.

Published in Great Britain in 1987 by
Muller, Blond & White Limited
62/65 Chandos Place,
London WC2N 4NW.

This is a Motovun publication.

British Library Cataloguing in Publication Data
Verstockt, Mark
    The genesis of form: from chaos to
    geometry
    1. Symbolism—History   2. Signs and
    symbols—History
    I. Title   II. De genesis van de vorm.
    English
    001.56   P99

    ISBN 0-584-11100-2
    ISBN 0-584-11109-6 Pbk

Printed and bound in Great Britain by R. J. ACFORD, CHICHESTER

CONTENTS

C'est que l'art se fait dans le monde des formes et non
dans la région indéterminée des instincts.
H. FOCILLON (*Vie des formes*)

Note We have deliberately kept the style of the illustrations as
neutral as possible, because any other more subjective style
would be less exact—and thus inappropriate to our intentions.

Our main consideration is to reproduce the structure of
the graphic sign as it appears in the different interpretations
of different cultures, in whatever form it might be used.

Generally, the drawings are accompanied by one or more
examples of cultures where the graphic sign can be found;
these may lie as far apart as prehistory and the 20th century.

Needless to say, completeness can never be achieved.

The drawings were done by Maarten van Severen; the
hand-drawn illustrations by Martine de Kesel.

THE GENESIS OF FORM

While it is helpful to make an inventory of all the aspects of a phenomenon, it is more important to look for a structure linking the components that serves to emphasize and clarify their evolution, interaction, influences, diffusion and interconnections. Our aim with this study in the field of signs and form has been to gain by analysis a better knowledge of the graphical material of communication, and thus to use it more efficiently and more consciously. The abstract, experimental art of the beginning of this century was constantly and clearly involved, whether consciously or unconsciously, in the search for a primeval means of expression, a return to the font of creativity. After the pretentious and prudish aestheticism of the 19th century, which banished all abstract and geometrical forms to the realm of decorative art, our century rediscovered these forms as valuable vehicles of expression, which, from their beginnings, they had always been. In the first half of the 20th century the Bauhaus (1919–33) and De Stijl (1917–32) in particular focused their attention on basic forms; the Russian Constructivists (1920) and the artists of Cercle et Carré (1930) and Abstraction Création (1931–36) followed. From then to the present, constructivist and concrete artists the world over have never ceased to include these primeval forms in their research (fig. 1).

Fig 1
Josef Peeters
Lino—1920

In the course of this study, points of contact with logographic, ideographic and pictographic communication could not be avoided, but beyond the formal aspect we were reluctant to enter these areas except where they might help elucidate the matter under consideration. At the same time, we have attempted to draw a distinction between forms without meaning, i.e. without reference to reality, and forms with a meaning, or *signs* (with a signifier and a signified); but sometimes this is untenable, since so-called *forms*, which should therefore have no meaning, appear in the end result to be able to function as signs, or to be so interpreted. So as not to introduce any new or academic terms, we propose to call the second group *signs* and the first group *abstract* signs or *forms*, or on some occasions *graphics* or *graphisms*. The latter is used as the term for a generalized graphic shape or element; a type of graphic rather than a specific graphic itself; and frequently the abstract, creative and 'primary' rather than the functional aspects of a drawn shape, form or sign. A square, for example, can clearly be called a form, whereas a segment of a line cannot. Both can have a symbolic meaning and thus are here called *signs*, but if they are regarded simply as designs, that is, without meaning, then a line segment should preferably be called an '*abstract*' *sign*, and a square rather an *abstract form*.

This is a broad area, and we have therefore restricted ourselves to the most elementary developments. When, however, we have been unable to resist the temptation (e.g., in respect of the human form: see page 126) to leave our designated path, we happily throw it in as a whimsical digression. We keep to our self-imposed limitations, however, by not, for example, attempting to examine faunal and floral ornamentation, based on the imitation of nature (figurative stylization), in any depth, despite touching occasionally on that aspect; this could form the subject of a separate study, even if it meant recapitulating the most primitive stages of graphical development.

It goes without saying that we are well aware of the many deficiencies of this book, and are certain that, for example, ethnologists, semiologists, theologists, psychologists and—why not?—metaphysicists would be well able to undertake a fuller examination within their own subjects, or, indeed, might have already done so. Our intentions were more concerned with morphology, but the abundance of symbolic, psychological, religious and other interpretations could not be ignored, and were helpful in achieving a better understanding of the development and original structure of signs and forms. Sign and form are extremely vital: tenacious on the morphological level, they hold their own through the centuries as their functions change, depending on the intentions of the manipulating individual and the period in which they are used. A knowledge of successive interpretations and symbolisms can only lead to a better understanding of morphology. Any attempt at completeness, however, would have resulted in an over-encyclopaedic work.

The schematicized, androgynous sign for a human being, for

example, develops in the course of history and from culture to culture, both in its appearance and in its significance. A similar development can also be observed with abstract signs and forms.

In today's concrete art, a circle is clearly a *circle* and a square is a *square*, but behind this circle and this square lie, historically speaking, *all* circles and squares, with the same morphological characteristics but different semantic qualities. Much as the concrete artist may have the intention of giving his language of forms the maximum autonomy, and may follow this intention, the historical relationship is still there. An understanding of the historical and cultural context is not indispensable to the artist of this century, but artists such as Klee, Kandinsky, Delaunay, van Doesburg and others have sought to broaden their knowledge of the phenomenon of form so as to strengthen the foundations of current art. We have found that, in the 20th century, a formal estrangement from the archaic signs, the archetypes in a Jungian sense, has been less great outside the field of art, too, than might at first sight be thought; does not the symbol-set of a computer, for example, contain enough primitive signs to support this

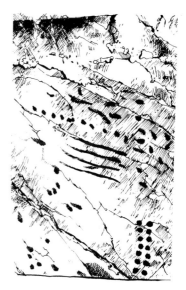

Fig 2
The meaning of the spots on the prehistoric rock walls (in the cave of Niaux, France) was clear to the cave-dwellers, but we can only guess at their purpose. However, the morphology is no different from the dots in modern communications systems.

Fig 3
Extract from the symbols catalogue of a computer company. Morphologically, there is no difference between symbols on the walls of caves such as Lascaux, France, for example, and these. Even in our century of high technology, man must still fall back on the same elementary graphics.

finding (figs. 2 and 3)?

Practically every author we have consulted has complained about the boundless scope of his subject and asked for indulgence in respect of limitations and deficiencies. We ask the same indulgence for the hypothetical and intuitive nature of some proposals. Our aim is to reconstruct a graphic development, to set up a hierarchy stretching from, let's say, scribbles and scratches to geometrical forms: circles, squares, triangles. We have attempted to chart the evolution of the proto-geometric sign, through the different stages between a (supposed) zero (chaos*) and the basic shapes (circle, square, triangle). In the process, we were trying to arrive at a scale of cultural values rather than a factual trend of historical evolution, which is no simple exercise, since too many factors affect the formal development.

We might assume, for instance, that a primitive tribe would first produce a graphic mark of left-sloping strokes (\\\\\) or right-sloping strokes (/////) and then, in a later stage of development, draw one over the other to produce a cross decoration (XXXXX). But this assumption is by no means certain. The tribe might have adopted the cross pattern from a neighbouring tribe, without passing through the stroke pattern first.

The motor linkage on the one hand, and imagination and invention on the other, however minimally present, are important factors in the development of primary signs and forms. Undoubtedly the whole process is rooted in an animistic experience of nature. We can therefore posit from the outset a definite relationship between communication by gesture and the primary sign. The gesture can itself become a sign. Thus we see that where gesture steps in when words are not enough, the same verbal impotence can give rise to signs. Gesture can strengthen the spoken word, give it power,

---

*Chaos—negative and positive finding harmony in darkness, according to the Cabbala—is a concept that can be considered on many levels. It means potential energy in the immaterial as well as the material sense; it contains a maximum as well as a minimum of information. We can say chaos is basically anti-order and anti-time: once we introduce a point into chaos, chaos ends; at that moment time and space are created and order exists. Chaos can only exist in opposition to order (and of course *vice versa*)—and in this book, where the thesis concerns the creation of order, the genesis of form, chaos is a most useful antithesis.

emphasize it; likewise the sign. Gestures can be the expression of deep emotions (aggression, sadness, despair ...) or of religio-cosmic aspirations (worship, invocation, conjuration, devotion ...), and signs themselves can indicate the same attitudes. We can extend this parallel as far as dance, where rhythm plays an important role; we can also discern this rhythm in the structures of signs (see Man and the Geometry of the Body, page 115). We further find that these primeval signs manifest themselves in more complex irrational, emotional, aesthetic or other processes, as well as in spontaneous graphical, serial or rhythmical applications, for example during ritual activities or playful/creative processes. It is also probable that actions and gestures in prehistoric ritual resulted in signs: for example, hand prints (the cave of El Castillo, Spain) or arrows drawn on representations of wild game (the caves of Niaux and Lascaux, France).

On a graphical level, we can subdivide signs into two categories: *open* signs and *closed* signs (if we apply this to Western script, we could say that the open signs comprise: C,E,F,G,H,I,J,K.L,M,N,S,T,U,V,W,X,Y,Z; and the closed signs: A,B,D,O,P,Q and R).

The primary *open* signs belong to a lower cultural level, and their execution makes minimal demands on the skill of the artist. The semantic input is likewise limited. They are produced with very few actions or movements of the hand: one (point, line), two (wedge), three (fork), several (zigzag). The *closed* signs are part of a higher cultural level, and the difficulty of their execution is greater than that of the primary open signs. Their production makes higher demands on the artist's awareness and requires a rational input: composition, relationships, correction, combination, judgement ... the movements are: one (circle), two (mandorla), three (triangle), four (square), several (polygon).

From an even higher cultural level derive the combinations of *open* + *closed* signs and *closed* + *closed* signs. In both cases we also find a double, plural, often complementary symbolism: Christ-and-the-disciples (cross-in-square), spirit-and-matter (circle-in-square). Even in the simpler open signs we can recognize a plural, frequently complementary symbolism: the cross (vertical + horizontal) unites male and female, life and death, yin and yang ...

Perhaps, as we trace the often uncertain path taken by the development of signs and forms, we could speak of 'haphazard creativity' (Lévi-Strauss in *La Pensée Sauvage*, calls it *bricol-*

age) to refer to the lack of technical competence with which the primitive artist, in his ignorance, nevertheless endeavours to give expression to what is in his mind. In fact, such an artist is not aware that there is any problem: he is simply producing something, and luck sees him through where his ability fails him. Over a very long period, which might cover generations, he will tend to improve and at the end of the process achieve some virtuosity. The technical handicaps to be overcome by the primitive artist, on the one hand, and his will to expression on the other, are evident in his work. Imitation of nature (mimesis) as an aid to drawing is rarely encountered, and the sole stimulus is the advancement of technical ability. Franz Boas in *Primitive Art* wrote:

> There is nothing to show the mere contemplation of nature or of natural objects develops a sense of fixed form. Neither have we any proof that a definite stylistic form develops as a product purely of the power of imagination of the workman, unguided by his technical experience which brings the forms into his consciousness. It is conceivable that elementary esthetic forms like symmetry and rhythm are not entirely dependent upon technical activities; but these are common to all art style; they are not specifically characteristic of any particular region.

It might be noted here that to draw parallels with the evolution of drawing skills in a child is not always as useful as it might at first seem, since this drawing comes about within a culturally determining pattern. That does not invalidate the fact that there are indeed clear parallels to be drawn, such as the pleasure in rhythms experienced by the child as he uses his fingers to mark a sheet of paper with dots of paint, or by, for instance, the Manon girl (western Ivory Coast) adding white spots to her blue-painted body before an initiation ritual (fig. 4). Another remarkable case of parallelism can be identified in the fact that the basic archetypal forms appear just as spontaneously in the drawings of children (cf. Rhoda Kellog, *What Children Scribble and Why*). But as Alfred Baader asserts in *Though This Be Madness*, drawings by the mentally ill also show a spontaneous reflection of what are called archetypal forms *originating in the collective unconscious* (fig. 5). It is indeed strange that few basic forms have their origin in direct imitation of nature (e.g., the sun-circle, the snail-spiral ...), although this certainly does occur, but rather in a motor-graphical activity, cosmic and magical in inspiration. It is possible that the products of this creative, spontaneous activity later get used as symbols and eventually as ornaments.

Fig 4
Manon girl (Ivory Coast) painted for the initiation rite: the body is painted blue and covered with white spots. Painting with the fingertips directly on to the body or another surface is very much a primary creative act. Children, too, find a great deal of pleasure in fingerpainting.

Fig 5
Drawing by a mental patient, Jules, in which the primeval marks (dots, lines, chequer patterns, spirals) are used as filling for the plain areas.

Technical experience and the acquisition of virtuosity have probably led to the general prevalence of the plane, the straight line and regular curves such as the circle and the spiral, for all these are of rare occurrence in nature, so rare indeed that they had hardly ever a chance to impress themselves upon the mind (Boas, *Primitive Art*).

Elsewhere, Boas frequently lays emphasis on the importance of motor play as the principal origin of sign language, with rhythm as the driving force and technical ability as a necessity, but with technical predetermination as a restriction. It is clear that societies with a greater rate of artistic production have a faster-developing and more varied armoury of forms at their disposal, as a consequence of intense artistic activity and specialization. In *Le Geste et la Parole*, A. Leroi-Gourhan says on the nature of primitive graphics:

Les opérations religieuses sont plus rarement figurées et les concepts métaphysiques font l'objet de représentations abstraites.

In contrast, S. Giedion asserts (*La Naissance de l'Art*):

Masques, créatures hybrides et êtres indéterminés sont des manifestations des premières tentatives de l'homme pour donner une forme à l'expérience religieuse.

Fig 6
Enrico Baj.—*Snake*
The snake, the living line, an undulating or coiled form, universal and with a strong appeal to the imagination, is frequently the source of undulating, zigzag or spiralling signs. But it can also be, and is more likely, that these signs originated in the motor activity of the hand, at the very primary stage, and only later took on a reference to the snake.

13

Fig 7
The fact that the four artists Malevich, Tschaschnik, Richard Allen and Aurélie Nemours divided surface space in a similar manner indicates, on the one hand, the obsession artists have for this strong horizontal and vertical combination, primeval form and sign and, on the other hand, the limitations of abstract thematics in which personal interpretation is the only variant.

It *can* happen that signs come about through an unconscious mimesis of forms in nature. But it is much more common for signs to take on *post factum* the meaning of similar phenomena in nature. Thus the spiral, in fact deriving from a spiralling, playful hand-movement, could be an unconscious aping of the coiled snake and originally have a totally different significance, e.g., *sun*, only to re-assume its reference to the snake much later. It is further possible that in this last stage the previous significance is lost or forgotten, or becomes coupled to the latest meaning (sun-snake).

In this context we should draw attention from the very outset to the limited nature of the graphics and forms developed by man, and of the possibilities for development available to the primitive designer, which can be laid at the door of various socio-cultural factors. But these limitations are not exclusive to the primitive designer/artist: we can also see the phenomenon of limited choice in folk art and decoration, and even in the art of our own century (fig. 7).

Signs originate in a different creative process from figuration. The primitive process that gives birth to abstract signs is in the first instance a motor one. Figuration arises from a mimetic process. Signs are closer to writing than what we would call 'artistic expression' (cf. Leroi-Gourhan).

The primitive draughtsman/sign-drawer has no aesthetic or formal anxieties: expression (cosmic, magical, religious) is important and, in so far as the degree of technical difficulty

may be very slight, the execution of the sign is a repeated attempt to achieve mastery of both the material on which the drawing is made and the instrument by which it is made. The *artistic* creative process, ending in the banality of a *l'art pour l'art* product, only gets under way very late in primitive and prehistoric cultures. In numerous cultures we can observe the development of a split between what we can call *writing* (making signs) on the one hand and *drawing* (artistic expression) on the other. It may also be that there is a continuing relationship between the two tendencies, as for instance in pictographic writing or in Chinese (bone-writing) calligraphy. What we call *writing*, including the pictographic varieties, is marked by a formalistic development. *Drawing* develops more freely.

Undoubtedly there are also obstacles of an extra-creative sort. We note, for example, that artistic production among the Eskimos is for the most part very small scale. This, of course, is due to the scarcity and small size of suitable materials: some seal-ivory, some pebbles, some bones... Naturally, this will have an influence on the quantity and quality of creativity. Central African tribes, on the other hand, are very highly productive, as a result of the manifold and abundant presence of easily workable woods. This natural stimulus certainly encourages variety of production and skill on the part of the artist. Here, geographic and climatic circumstances clearly have an influence on the possibilities for

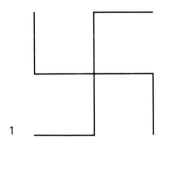

1

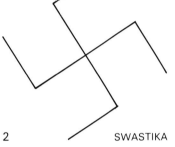

2   SWASTIKA

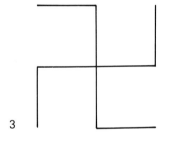

3

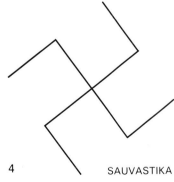

4   SAUVASTIKA

cultural development.

We can also mention in this connection a steady, inevitable, compelling evolution towards certain universal archetypal forms. We thus see the hooked cross of the sun wheel (Anglo-Saxon: *fylfot* = many-footed, tetraskelion), either right-handed or left-handed, originating spontaneously within separate cultures on separate continents: among the Cretans, the Greeks, the Germanic tribes, the Pre-Columbian Indians, the Eskimos, the Indians, the Tibetans, the Africans—but with a completely different starting point in each case, and frequently a different symbolic value, here a sign of luck, there a sign of misfortune. Yet, at the same time, there are some areas where this sign remains totally unknown: for instance in Central Africa, in Zoroastrianism in Mesopotamia. Certainly the dissemination of this sign from India was appreciable, but equally certainly this was not the sole source of all swastika signs throughout the world, as the diffusionists would claim.

It is well established that travel was widespread even in earliest historic times, that an overseas barter trade was carried on with distant peoples, that emigration took place, sometimes enforced because return proved impossible, as a result of ocean currents, for example. It thus came about that ways of life, (death) rituals and a number of signs too were transported by chance far from their origins. But it is hardly acceptable to suppose that the peoples among whom these cultural forms settled were not themselves already enjoying a secure cultural development, even if this was more primitive than that of the donor. Thus, serious researchers are baffled by the fact that some signs showing similarity with Breton ones are encountered in Ireland, but others belonging to the same armoury of signs are not. Why only these and not the others? Did the seafarers from Brittany acquire or influence certain rock graphics? This would be perfectly possible. There are similarities between the arc or bow graphics of Gavr'inis and those of Loughcrew and Knowth, which give support to the donor hypothesis. But in that case, what of the equally apparent similarities with graphics in Africa and America?

Eon MacWhite (*Estudios sobre las relaciones Atlanticas de la Peninsula Hispanica en la Edad del Bronce*, Madrid, 1951) asserts that the Western European spiral could have travelled from Egypt via Malta, back to the North African mainland and from there to Gran Canaria, finally settling in the Atlantic part of Europe. Then there is the even more complicated story of the trek onward from Atlantic Europe to Ireland, northern

England and Scotland, and from there to Scandinavia.

In our endeavours to understand primitive forms and signs, we have been struck time and again by their moving powerlessness, their humble simplicity, their honest graphical quality. Where earlier periods (notably the 19th century) did not even attempt to understand them and branded them barbarian products or ethnological curiosities, we study them with the aim of finding in them the origins of art, the primeval stage of human communication. We compare prehistoric graphics with the forms of expression of present-day primitive cultures, and attempt, through these comparisons, to find analogies. It is evident that the prehistoric archetypes had their origin in different geographical, climatological and socio-cultural circumstances than the pictograms of contemporary Africans or American Indians. Yet clear agreements are demonstrable, which give support to certain deductions.

The mainsprings behind the primitive artist's creativity are many, but must always be sought in his primeval condition: his attitude to the unknown, to the cosmos, to nature and natural phenomena, his emotions, his fears, his pastimes, his sexuality... He was certainly influenced also by the slowness of processes surrounding him, the unhurried rhythm of life, the surplus of time, the tedium of winter or of long periods of rain.

As to the indications of time, it is difficult to set estimates. Signs and forms sometimes evolve extremely slowly; often centuries pass before the next stage of development or the next combination is achieved. For this slowness various reasons, sometimes contradictory, can be offered: the sedentary condition (conservative, though at the same time frequently very creative); migration (too little rest to allow evolution, the continuing use of existing elements, products always to be carried on the journey); economy (the hardness of the living conditions, which demanded too much energy for there to be any spare for creativity); domination by other peoples; the climate... A strong traditional sense of style, which is not unusual in primitive peoples, can be a powerful brake on the artistic evolution of the individual artist, and equally on that of the group. We cannot say, however, that the artist merely copies; rather that he keeps, slavishly and almost without variation, to the familiar patterns and schemes.

Evolution is thus slow, the inventory of achievement

Fig 8
Ashanti gold weights
The gold weights decorated with geometrical forms are less popular than weights with human and animal images, in their inexhaustible variety, and it is probable that these forms (squares, diamonds, swastikas, pyramids, stars, combs ...) were adopted, probably from designs that travelled with traders to the Gold Coast.

Fig 9
Pot with dactylograms
This 2nd century B.C. clay pot (Royal Museums of Art and History, Brussels) is decorated in a primitive style by the marks of fingers pressed into the clay. It is possible that the surface decoration was intended to prevent the pot slipping from the fingers when drawing water. However, in the rhythmic manner in which the decoration is laid out we can also see an attempt to give the pot an individual, personal and aesthetic character.

generally minimal. Sometimes one or other factor, difficult to pinpoint, will introduce itself, with the result that, within a short period of time, the designer/artist does invent new forms or brings novel and different combinations to the fore. Some kind of process of acceleration manifests itself thanks to some special talent, the genius of an individual or a change in the socio-cultural structure within the group, or a refreshing new *élan* after a period of stagnation. A curious thing is that some peoples, such as certain African pygmies—in spite of their, however slight, contact with other tribes—have never developed a graphic activity beyond the secondary stage of two lines (e.g., on their bows). Dance, too, has remained binary and extremely primitive among the pygmies: one foot raised and one on the ground. Their music comprises one high note and one low note. In contrast to this, they had—in relation to the tribes among whom they lived—a highly developed technology: compared with the hunting implements of other groups, who were culturally further developed, their arrows flew far more precisely, and were stronger and more functional (their arrows had flights of animal skin, a foot at the back which made better contact with the bow-string and, at the point, sharp barbed hooks).

Surprising, too, is the discovery that the cross shape was unknown in Asia Minor until the Cretans imported it at the time of their raids on the mainland; that Greek slaves imported a wealth of previously unknown forms into Rome; that the geometrical forms on the gold weights of the Ashanti of West Africa (fig. 8) probably travelled with the gold and were introduced to the Ashanti by that route. This supports our assertion that so-called archetypal, simple, cultural elements (such as · — | /\ +) did not arise by themselves and as a matter of course within *all* prehistoric, pre-literate and even historical social patterns. Sometimes it was war, raids, migrations, (slave) trading or colonization that dispersed signs and forms across the continents.

Certain peoples achieved speedy evolution on the craft level (utensils, clothing, textiles, weapons, adornment, ritual objects ...), with highly advanced functionalism in the shape of the objects, but remained very primitive in their symbolism and ornamentation (lines, crosses, dots ...) (fig. 9).

We do know that some cultures, such as some Pre-Columbian ones (fig. 10, a–b), developed the human or animal figure almost to anatomical perfection, or at least set up

Fig 10 a
Maya statuette (Guatemala).
This human figure was modelled in clay according to reasonably accurate anatomical rules, but has been decorated very clumsily. Was the figure modelled by one artist and the graphics added by another?

Fig 10 b
Mayan figurine
This contemporary statuette from Michoacam, in the Chupicuaro style (pre-Classical, 1200–500 B.C.), has a much more primitive anatomical structure but a strong geometrical and sophisticated decoration.

canons for the representation of men and animals that evidenced a sure sense of relationships, and we can add that, alongside this, abstract decoration stagnated at a markedly elementary, restricted stage. Perhaps we might posit that in many cases the two were the work of different artists: one produced the figuration and another the abstract decoration. Or, alternatively, that the simple abstract signs were a sort of magical completion of the figuration; this probably does in fact apply to the marks over and beside the animal drawings of Lascaux (fig. 10, c).

After the production of weapons of defence and implements for hunting and fishing, ceramics and basket-weaving were the oldest trades by which man sought to satisfy his elementary needs. Baskets and pots no doubt originally took shape in imitation of familiar receptacles in nature: the cupped hand, the scallop shell, the leaf, the gourd, the bamboo... But occasionally these originals were forgotten, and from easily worked and re-worked material (reeds, clay) freely developed shapes were produced, answering to a very precise functionality. From the technique itself there arose, unconsciously, as if growing spontaneously from the co-ordination of hand and eye, structures and forms which could be the occasion for new, unsuspected possibilities of expression. The craftsman's product became, as it were, the training ground of the aspiring designer. In the vertical and horizontal structure and in the rhythms of the weave, patterns came into being—at first, possibly by accident—through the use of reeds or fibres of different colours: squares, angles, blocks, steps,

Fig 10 c
Cave painting, Lascaux
Were the drawing of the horse and the addition of the mysterious signs (arrows, animal trap?) one operation?

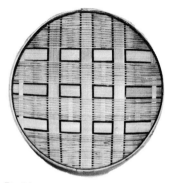

Fig 11
Present-day Italian folk basket-weave, in which we can see clearly how the use of differently coloured reeds produces geometric effects.

Fig 12
Makiritare Indian basketweave. The techniques used in making this product have developed schematic (stylized) representations of still-recognizable figures. These also appear, in a further abstracted form, in carvings, necklace beads and metalwork, where they may only just recall the original figures. All staircase forms in primitive art derive from woven originals.

diagonals, crosses... Later, the reeds would be coloured deliberately, to achieve greater variation in the patterns or structures (fig. 11). The sensitive, soft clay used by the potter was an excellent potential vehicle for all kinds of line-drawn designs. The jug or dish built up from rolls of clay already carried in it the structure of the spiral, the circle, the continuous line, the undulating line...

We see the theory growing from the practice of production (craftsmanship), and subsequently settling in the imagination of the producer, where it is stored, to be applied later in other graphical disciplines. This means that we must postulate clear interaction between the different disciplines: the herringbone technique from weaving, for example, is imitated in pottery and carving; the horizontal and vertical lines of warp and weft are copied on the walls of the cave or the hut; the horizontal-and-vertical design of the fishnet (chequer pattern) is transferred to dishes... This can even be ascribed to a kind of cultural laziness. For example, at the outset earthenware is set in the bottom of baskets for baking, and takes on the pattern of the woven material. In a later stage the craftsman will imitate the same structure in separately made pots, pitchers, dishes, and cast or beaten metalwork. Often a variety of geometric schematicization of figurative motifs (man, animal, plant) comes about through imitation of these figurative forms as they appear in woven fabric or basketwork (fig. 12), which may extend to abstraction that is no longer recognizable.

But this, in conjunction with what we have said above, indicates an already advanced degree of cultural development. In some American Indian tribes, the weaving of headbands, neckbands and belts is said to be an experimental medium where variants on the traditional signs are tried out. In other tribes, conversely, it is the weaving of blankets, baskets and mats that is important for creativity. Tribes are said to specialize in one or other industrial product, to use them as a bartering commodity in their relations with other tribes. This can lead to forms and signs being adopted by other tribes and being used in techniques removed from the original one, and also to the signs being given different and new meanings, though without discarding the original meanings. Boas is quite right when he speaks of the influence of trading on the development of graphics and forms: this influence can scarcely be over-estimated. But against this he considers entirely hypothetical the position of those who attempt to trace *all* forms and structures to a craft-technical source.

It can happen that the women who produce the ceramics also add the designs (decoration) on them*; that the smith—who frequently has important socio-religious functions in the tribe—also fashions the images for ritual occasions; that the medicine man is also the village artist... In the most primitive cultures there was no specialized *artist* function. When differentiation of function does come about, this marks an important phase in the evolving social process. On the one hand there is craft—the production of the functional utility object. On the other side there appears *free* art—at this stage, nearly always subordinate to the dictates of a governing or priestly caste using art for the sake of prestige, or as a component of a programme to sustain its power. It can thus come about at this stage that art becomes decoration, ornament, frills, or art for art's sake.

It is not unusual to find two, three or more primary graphic elements brought together on one piece of primitive ceramics. While certainly indicating that we are dealing with a sure sense of invention—the combination of different elements—this must still be regarded as a combination of miscellaneous influences, or an achievement by the primitive artist that arises from his own research into form. But it can also happen that we observe a sudden growth of graphical variety within a large cultural group, which results in a fruitful evolution of style within the sections of the group. Thus we may suppose that during a period of severe drought in the area of the Pueblo Indians, for example, a wide variety of symbols came into being, perhaps highly varied in form and inspiration, some referring to rain, some to its consequences (fertility). This may well be connected with the complexity of the message or story. Wall decorations have been recorded by Mallery* that present a complete armoury of the primeval signs (Inhamun, Brazil; Owens Valley, California). The universality of this phenomenon, which can be seen in practically all

---

*It is not only in present-day primitive cultures that the women carry out the artistic work for the group (family or tribe). It is very probable that they also did so in the earliest period of *Homo sapiens*. Is it not an elegant position to maintain that women fashioned pots according to their own physiognomy and hence their own psyche, in sensuous and elegant shapes (Hoernes)? If it was also women who scraped the signs in the soft clay, we might conclude that women not only created the trade of artist, but art itself. *Mater vitae et mater artis...*

Fig 13
Bobo mask (Upper Volta).
This *do* or ancestor mask shows a wealth of different signs, all strongly geometric in design. Such pronounced feeling for geometric forms is found in many African tribes, notably the Dogon, the Bamiléké, and the Mangbetu ... (collection of the author).

primitive cultures, could be the subject of a separate comparative study (fig. 13). We can also refer in passing to a number of phenomena of Western culture of the early Middle Ages, such as the tympanum of the church at Cortrat, in Loiret (fig. 14) and that of the Great Rollington church in Oxfordshire—two vivid examples of accumulations of primitive signs.

In fact, it is especially absorbing to observe primitive man occupied in some graphical activity for its own sake, such as adding in spontaneous play a design to earthenware, simply to decorate the object or to give it a personalized character, without even the clear aim of producing a sign or symbol. It is particularly fascinating when the manipulated form or design is of a kind that does not demand the slightest specialized artistic skill (scratches, dots, stipples, lines, crosses...), so that we can observe the maker's sense of motor activity and rhythm, or see him satisfy his ambition to build structures, with inborn intense, pure sensitivity.

Signs and primary forms may be elements of a game (fig. 15). But it is most likely that the game (whether purely for play or as a magical/divinatory activity) is the origin of the sign (as, for example, the casting of rune sticks would produce the rune).

A connection between rhythm and emotion was established by Jung. Mastery of the mechanisms of rhythm and structure leads to proficiency in form. In praise of rhythm, Michel Seuphor writes in his *La tendance à la répétition des signes géométriques simples dans l'art contemporain* (published by Convergences, Paris-Nantes, 1982, under the title *Autour du Cercle et du Carré*):

Nous sommes rythme avant tout autre chose; nous naissons rythme, et ce n'est que bien longtemps après que nous naissons à la pensée. Mais la pensée est elle-même issue de ce rythme, elle en est en quelque sorte l'efflorescence extrême. Voilà sans doute la raison pour laquelle le rythme et la pensée se comprennent si bien. Ils se nourissent l'un l'autre, en quelque sorte de leur substance mutuelle.

It is quite possible that such rhythmic *sign exercises* or *structural experiments* were only much later introduced to a

---

*Mallery, Garrick, *Pictographs of the North American Indians; a preliminary paper*. Tenth Annual Report of the Bureau of Ethnology to the Secretary of the Smithsonian Institution, 1888–89.

magical, ritual or ordinary system of communication. Rationality is never the rule in the chain of development of signs and forms. But no doubt this is an aspect of human genius.

When overproduction occurs, resulting in a higher level of general ability, we see the appearance of a looser graphical style, and the artist, as it were, *writes* the signs. At this point all the characteristics of handwriting can be seen (personal traits, sloppiness, fluency ...), and motor activity becomes once again an important element in the creative process.

Often we see the primitive craftsman append his personal sign (signature) to his product. It may also be that this sign is the symbol of the group: the tribe or the place of work, for example. It is as if he (or the group) desires the product to be recognized as a personal creation by means of the proprietary sign, and as if the artefact, marked by the signature, is given extra protection, so that any imitation would mean an infringement of the personality of the maker (or the group). This mark, identifying the maker, is itself an identity.

When a culture opts for an alphabetic, linear system of writing, this results in a differentiation within the communication of the group. On the one hand, the pictogram will evolve within very formal limits from the drawing; on the other, the

Fig 14
On the early-Romanesque tympanum of the church at Cortrat (Loiret, France) we can see a battery of primitive signs, surrounding a creation story interwoven with mazes, as if expressing the continuing struggle between pagan and Christian influences.

Fig 15
Children's drawings on a wall in Fez (Morocco). This game is usually played on the ground, like our hopscotch, but sometimes the children draw the game's pattern on a wall as a graffito.

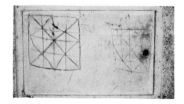

drawing will embark on an autonomous evolution and have a totally new function. True, a large number of symbols continue in existence, or are included in the script, but as a result of the advent of the *written* word these will slowly but surely lose their power.

In the Far East, however, a picture-writing script has come into being in which the link with drawing is maintained. The practice of calligraphy has specialized exponents and masters, who are usually painters and artists as well. It also comes about that, when a master calligrapher is asked by an artist to add calligraphy to a painting, to complete it aesthetically, the calligraphy will truly reflect and complement the spirit of that painting: a meeting of calligraphy and painting in one whole. In its essence, calligraphy is just as unique as painting, with the same subjective and personal qualities. This is confirmed by the fact that many calligraphers (Chinese, Japanese, Arabic) sign their characters as autonomous works of art. Frequently the calligraphy and the picture (painting or drawing) are produced in one operation: the writing accompanies the picture, or vice versa. Sometimes the calligraphy runs into the drawing, so that we have difficulty distinguishing where the writing ends and the drawing begins (cf. Roland Barthes, *L'Empire des Signes*).

In *Ryakuga Haya Oshie* (Rapid Reading in Simplified Characters) (1814), Hokusai redraws a scene with two men chatting as an example of calligraphy (*hiragana*). A swarm of dragonflies flows over into the accompanying text, with the aim of establishing the relationship between the two graphical genres: calligraphy grew out of drawing (painting); or: drawing (painting) grew out of calligraphy.

La calligraphie... intermédiaire entre la peinture et la poésie. Le peintre et le calligraphe se servent du même instrument: le pinceau... Il n'y a pas de discontinuité entre les traits peints et les traits calligraphiés. (François Cheng in *La Traversée des Signes*).

Writing and image are thus one. It can be seen from this that within these cultures the graphical quality of the written characters is in fact very important for communication. Unfortunately that is no longer the case in our alphabetized cultures—a fact which may certainly be regarded as an impoverishment of communication.

In our Western culture we are familiar with, for example, Gothic calligraphy, but the quality of that writing was very formal-aesthetic and could, indeed, be a specialized occupa-

Chinese calligraphy in the Tsau-Tse style: to do, make, write, work, act.

Dans ma chambre, ou, pour mieux dire : dans ma carrée, la carrée étant, le châssis d'un lit et rrellent deux rondes de musique, dans ma currée pour la charade,

tion, drawing remaining a separate specialized area. In our society, art and writing are irrevocably parted. It is with evident nostalgia that 20th-century artists turn to calligraphy: Mathieu, Hartung, Alechinsky, Tobey, Dotremont (fig. 16), Michaux...

It is part of our intention to stress that the primeval sign or form is universal; that it has been in use, an attainment of man and a property of society, in all eras, and thus, needless to say, in our computer society too, often with the same metaphysical function as in furthest antiquity; and that the semantic and graphical usefulness of these signs and forms is not subject to any attrition. Here we need only call in evidence the morphology of heraldry, military insignia, signs for all forms of transport, symbols for typewriters and computers, the language of mathematics and the exact sciences ... and, last but not least, the art of the 20th century.

History adds new meanings to the *immanent*, *archetypal* and *universal* signs, but these do not destroy the previous symbolism as a result. Signs may fall into disuse, sometimes for very long periods, and similarly return from oblivion to sudden prominence, as if from a collective, cosmic memory;

Fig 16
Christian Dotremont.
Logogram (1978).
A member of the Cobra group, Dotremont was particularly known for his poetic, active logograms. In common with his colleague Alechinsky, he regretted the absence of a calligraphic tradition in Western culture and clearly took inspiration from the East.

Western calligraphy (1601)

or they may disappear for good. Sometimes we see symbols decay to banal signs, or signs take on the function of a symbol. The interpretation of that symbolism (*le signifié*) will be dependent horizontally on the cultural period and the cultural pattern in which it is manifest, and vertically on the level at which it is (demagogically) manipulated within the culture (by magic, alchemy, religion, art . . .). The fact that the cross, with its cosmic, magic and religious meanings, was afterwards used in mathematics, in computer symbolism or as an element of ornament, changes absolutely nothing as regards the primeval meaning of that sign. There is simply a difference in level.

Often we find—as with the North American Indians—that the meaning of a sign changes from tribe to tribe, and even that each artist within the tribe, according to the context in which it is put, may attach a different meaning to the sign, because in this case no formal relationship exists between the form and what it symbolizes. Thus, for the Arapaho Indians, the horizontal double-axe sign with a vertical line through the point of contact can mean not so much *butterfly* as *star* (5,1.), but a cross (5,2.) and a diamond (5,3.) can also mean *star*, while a coloured-in diamond is *man* (human being) (5,4.). With the Pomo Indians, a triangular structure means *butterfly* for the northern and eastern groups and, for the central group, *arrowheads* (5,5.).

The manipulation of the abstract language of signs can be so individual that the act of drawing has meaning only for the artist, and even his immediate neighbourhood does not understand it. This would be the case with some prehistoric Indian tribes in East California, Nevada or Monterey, who had little figuration, and whose extensive armoury of signs largely consisted of geometric marks, which were very probably used to represent highly abstract and individually conceived ideas.

We take too little account of the important function of elementary conventional signs in our daily life. Think for a moment of the compelling effect a mandatory traffic sign has upon us. Only then is it brought home to us (when we stop) how insidiously, by a Pavlovian response, a sign can influence the pattern of our behaviour. We have seen men follow a sign in their thousands, as if following an obsession, or as if in an apocalyptic vision, to meet their death and destruction: crusaders behind the cross, Muslims behind the crescent, Nazis behind the swastika, Italy's fascists behind the fasces. . . We can see clearly how the *symbol* now becomes *reality*, making possible the substitution of one for the other; where

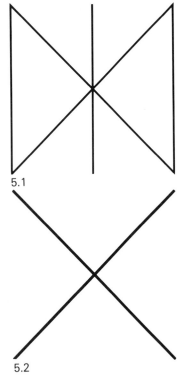

5.1

5.2

one is seen, the other is understood.

In prehistoric and primitive cultures it was the initiates, the priests, the priest-kings, the tribal chiefs, the magicians, the artists, who carried out the demagogic manipulation of the signs and who were the custodians of this form of communication within the society. This is also how they contrived to maintain their position against the non-initiates and to command respect. They had power.

The Benin of West Africa know the power of the sign very well. In this tribe it is always the king, and he alone, who is permitted to incise the tattoo motifs: he has power over the signs. Sometimes, as for example with the Ashanti, also of West Africa, the king, who is proprietor and custodian of the signs, distributes them to his subjects or notables, as a sign of gratitude or as a present. On the death of the owner, the signs were burned with his corpse, since they were so bound to the person that they could not be transferred to his heir; the sign being like the profoundest ego of the possessor.

In the cultures of India, too, the shaman or medicine man was the effective possessor of the signs; he alone knew their meaning, and it is clear that the interpretation varied from individual to individual. Possession of the signs and the hidden knowledge of their meaning also guaranteed the shaman's power and influence.

In many African and Indian tribes the aim of body-painting and of the designs on warriors' shields was to make an impression on the adversary. The sign became a talisman, a weapon, a defence; the primitive fighter recognized the power of the sign (magic) and believed in its protection and its influence on the enemy.

In our Western culture, man manipulates (and is manipulated by) signs in religion, magic, politics, ideology: the cross, the crescent, the swastika, the Cross of Lorraine, runes, the Star of David, the hammer and sickle, the triangle, dividers or compasses, the circle, the circle with a cross... Through the strong, condensed power of the economical graphical design of the sign on the one hand and the object to which it refers on the other, a kind of magical, compelling power is exercised over the reader, like the effect of a modern traffic sign with an unambiguous meaning. In cultures without writing, the sign is manipulated in a more complex manner, with added compactness resulting from greater spontaneity and directness. Of course, tradition plays a not insignificant role, and the consumption of the sign is far more evident there than in our

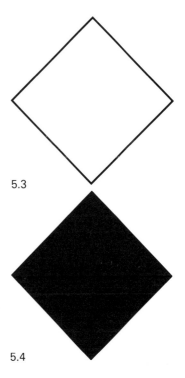

5.3

5.4

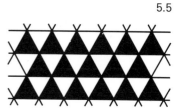

5.5

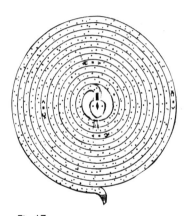
Fig 17
Detail of a Hopi sand drawing.

Fig 19
Cuneiform script from the palace of Darius (Persepolis).

alphabetized cultures.

We can agree with Dr. C. W. Verhoeven:

Not only usage, but tradition too makes the symbol banal.

Long before the sign lost its meaning, became desemanticized and gained the function of an ornament or an element within an ornamental graphic design (in which case we can speak of a degradation), it was used by man to communicate with the cosmic realm, or to give expression to his inner fears and tensions. Only much later was it to become a vulgarized means of communication between individuals. It is far too simplistic to maintain that an artist or craftsman, responding simply to the challenge of a blank surface which needs to be filled (*horror vacui*), draws simple graphical, optical effects on it, starting from such beginnings as order, symmetry, logic and clarity. Without wishing to minimize the part played by playful intent and chance, we believe that the processes that gave rise to the sign and to drawing in the earliest stages of *Homo sapiens graficus* were much more complex. The *horror vacui* may indeed provide a powerful stimulus to play, but it is an insufficient explanation, given the complexity of primitive creative processes.

In primitive cultures, every activity is ordered, everything has a purpose, every action, every sign, every image; a value-free phenomenon is very rare. Decoration for decoration's sake is most uncommon in early cultures, unless it is a manifestation of decadence, which has not prevented such serious researchers as MacAlister (1921) from warning us that:

... it would be absurd to read symbolism into every scratch on the surface of a pot; but we must always be prepared for the possibility that marks which to us seem merely decorative were at one time capable of a more recondite explanation. The key of this explanation is however lost, all but certainly, for ever; and we are therefore obliged to draw a rather arbitrary line between devices which we may reasonably consider as symbolic and those which may be treated as pure ornament.

Of great importance for a sign's vitality (charge of energy) is the graphical/technical quality with which it is executed: shape, positive-and-negative effect (*chiaroscuro*), symmetry, both top-bottom and left-right (*gemini*), asymmetry, verticalism, horizontalism, diagonalism, rhythm, counter-rhythm, movement, direction (centrifugal/centripetal), open or closed form... This does not mean that the sign must have an intrinsically sound technical execution in order to function in an optimal manner, but that the manner in which it is done must suit the aim in the maker's mind; whether this be explosive, aggressive, suggestive, spontaneous, meditative, ascetic, sacred, erotic, playful, rational, aesthetic, magical or decorative. It is inevitably difficult to put this into words, because of the subjective character of both the message contained and the observer's readiness to provide an interpretation. The magic graphics drawn with sand by the Navajo Indians, adopted by the Hopi (fig. 17), have a different expression from the structural, stacked walls of a Mixtec palace (fig. 20); brush-drawn calligraphic texts of Chinese or Japanese poets (fig. 18) have a different intensity from cuneiform letters pressed into clay tablets (fig. 19). A swastika dripping with tar on a collaborator's housefront (fig. 21b) has a different character from the same symbol on the triumphal banners of the Olympic Games of 1936 (fig. 21a).

In dealing with primitive signs and forms, there is only a minimal distinction to be made between the symbols of darkest prehistory and those of historical times, because the degree of difficulty involved in their production is very low and their origin remains the same universal and archetypal mind, bound to no specific era. Thus, the graphic quality of a circle scratched or painted on the walls of a prehistoric cave shows no significant formal difference to the graphic quality of a circle drawn by an African or Indian medicine man on some religious object; and equally insignificant are the differences between these and similar graphics from the Middle Ages or

Fig 18
Calligraphy (Japan).

Fig 20
Zapotec palace at Mitla (Mexico, 12th century A.D.) shows elaborate geometric patterns in the structural design of interior walls.

from modern times. The principal distinction, however, seems to be that man (the individual, but also the group) tends to develop fluency of execution, which evolves at a faster or slower pace according to the influences of external factors, passing from rough attempts and more formal exercises through virtuosity to decadence.

We can state that once a certain degree of proficiency has been reached, new forms and combinations of forms are more easily evolved. The discovery or coming into fashion of complicated systems is not necessarily a reason for the more primitive signs to be allowed to fall into disuse. The dot or the scratch remained in use, as intricate ornaments, for example, when imitated basketwork and knots made their entrance in the primitive armoury of signs. It is evident that the phenomenon changes fundamentally when the form becomes a product of geometric study or technical/mechanical production such as stamping with a roller seal (fig. 22). But the formal basis remains constant, and the form does not lose its usefulness: a circle remains a circle. In this case the manipulation may also change fundamentally, depending on the communication pattern and the interpretation, which in turn is dependent on the information (knowledge) of the individual or the group to which the message is directed.

The re-evaluation of basic forms and signs in art carried out during this century had such importance because it implied a totally different attitude to the business of art, and because at the same time new and revolutionary techniques were

Fig 21 (a) and (b)
Left: The triumphal swastikas on the building constructed for the Olympic Games in Berlin (1936), in a design borrowed from the Bauhaus.
Right: Swastika in a political street sign.

necessary for the production of a work of art.

These primeval signs and forms appear coincidentally at the same time as new technological possibilities, which art is quick to put to use. We see Mondrian, technically still very traditional, evolving out of Cubism. The Russian Constructivists took their inspiration from icons and folk art. Closer to home, after World War II, the forms of expression of many avant-garde artists were determined and stimulated by new, non-conventional materials (plastics, synthetic textiles ...) and techniques (silk-screen printing, spray-guns, lasers, computers ...). Now, an art product can be the result of a rational process (*pure image*) or of an intuitive choice. What we see, in fact, is a revolution in the entire morphology of art. The primeval forms—for so long banned from free art and relegated to the field of simple decoration—have become the basic elements of one of the most important and most diversified forms of artistic expression of our century: abstract art. It was the task of this art to revalue the primeval forms and rid them of their banality, by giving them once more a graphical, expressive and/or metaphysical content, along with a new function.

With *The Genesis of Form* we set out to provide a better insight into this language of forms, both by studying their primeval morphological metamorphosis and pointing out historical, archaeological and ethnological meanings, and by drawing attention to these forms where they occur in the art of our century.

Fig 22
Vase decorated with roller seal. The character of a graphic design changes whenever it is transferred to a pressing or stamping technique, as for example on this Bronze Age vase (Royal Museums of Art and History, Brussels).

CHAPTER I

TOWARDS A PRIMAL SIGN

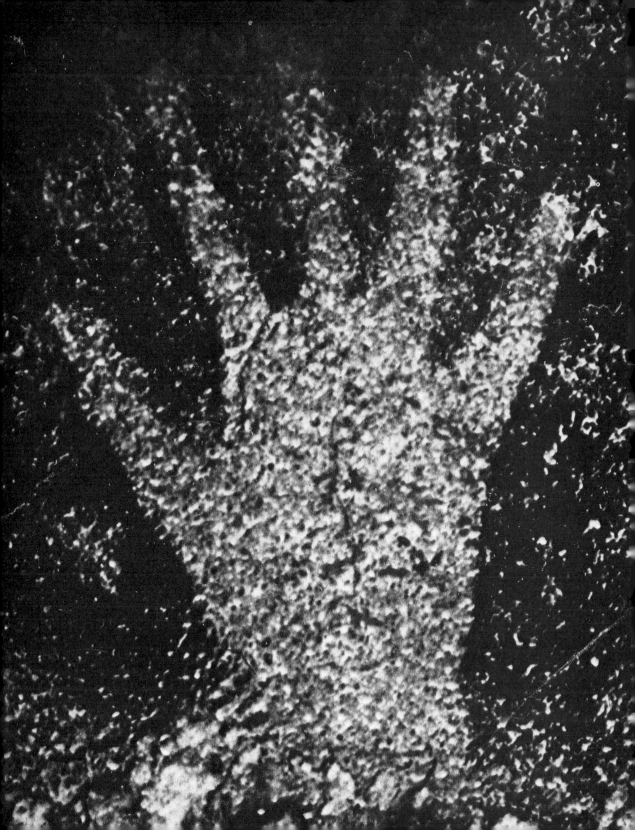

IMPRINTS OF THE BODY

Imprints of parts of the body (hands, feet, fingers, lips, faces, genitals . . .) feature not only in the world of the child and the life of the mentally disturbed: they are evident in all civilizations from the darkest primeval era up to the present day, as a primary manifestation of human creativity and an elementary pictographic communication. At a more developed stage, we see the parts of the body painted or drawn, usually in simple outline (Valcamonica, Italy) but sometimes filled in with all kinds of symbols (Tantrism). In primitive art, we seldom have an accurate observation and rendering of the human body or its parts. Occasionally the lines of the hands are observed and reproduced (e.g., the cave-drawings of Rejimkoojik) or the detail of the body is sketched in (e.g., the cave-drawings of Tassili, Algeria).

The commonest prints are those of the hand, that implement of implements (Aristotle), a powerfully emotive instrument of symbolism and expression. The hand can represent aggression or benediction, righteousness or power. With spread fingers (rays), it symbolizes the sun. The left hand is 'Yin' and weak, the right hand 'Yang' and strong. When man imprints his hand on a surface, he projects his deepest self, his ego. The hand *is* the man (S. Giedion).

Why did the dwellers of the caves of Oaxaca (Mexico), or those of Gargas (Hautes-Pyrenées, France) (fig. 23), Monte del Castillo (Spain) or central Australia, imprint mutilated hands* (fig. 24) on the walls of their abodes, sometimes in red and sometimes in black? Was it some kind of ritual? The exorcism of unfriendly spirits? The staking of territorial rights and ownership? Or was it a mark of aggression against the space itself? The language of people unable to express themselves in other ways? According to Herbert Kuhn,

*Did these damaged hands result from ritual mutilations? Or were they merely conventional hand signs?

Fig 24
Prints of mutilated hands on a rock wall.

Fig 23
Hand-print in Gargas cave (Hautes-Pyrenées, France.
The hand—the implement of implements—has always been an obsession for mankind. No two hands are the same. A hand is as individual and representative as a face. It is possible to read a hand. A hand-print is like a portrait, a print of the person himself.

Fig 25
1. A Fatimah-hand cut in zinc (modern Egypt). In Moslem countries the Fatimah hand is a widespread talisman; it can be found on houses, cars, horse harnesses, dresses, and jewels.
2. Fatimah hand on a horse harness (Egypt).
3. A hand-print on a wall in Fez (Morocco).

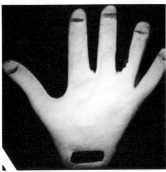

handprints are the oldest form of painting in the world.

Two types of handprints are found in prehistory. In positive print, the hand is dipped in pigment (blood, ochre or manganese) and applied to the wall. In the negative print, the hand is pressed flat against the wall and a brush or bundle of twigs is used to sprinkle pigment around it; sometimes colour is sprayed from the mouth. Less common is the linear or drawn hand. The hand is applied to the surface and the outline is etched around it with a sharp instrument. Only very occasionally in primitive and prehistoric cultures is the hand cut out of materials such as leather or bark. Another variation is the freely styled painted hand. In the case of the American Indian tribes, handprints on the clothes of a warrior are a mark of courage and prestige, signifying that he has killed one or more of his enemies.

In Islam, the printed or drawn hand is a reminder of the five precepts or pillars of belief: pilgrimage, fasting, prayer, confession of faith and charity. The Fatimah hand (fig. 25) brings luck. Fatimah was the eldest daughter of the prophet, one of the four perfect women. Each finger of the hand represents one member of the family: the thumb, Mohammed; the index finger, Fatimah; the middle finger, her husband Ali; the ring finger and little finger, her sons Hassan and Hussein; the little finger also signifies virtue. In Islam—as in, for example, the case of the Berbers—the hand is still the symbol of power and authority, guaranteeing protection against the evil eye.

In the Cabbala the letter Yod (ᐟ) has the mysterious hieroglyphic meaning of hand. The open hand symbolizes the microcosm: the four fingers are the material elements (Yod: air, Heh: fire, Vau: water, Heh: earth). The thumb is Shin: spirit. Yod equals ten (the ideal number), the sum of two hands.

Everywhere, even in our own culture, the hand appears as a symbol of malediction or protection, in magic and in folk customs: the evil hand, the hand of the devil, the hand that averts evil or illness.

Jung ascribes to the hand a generative meaning.

In the dolmen of Le Petit-Mont (Le Morbihan, France), two footprints were found. Did the prehistoric cave-dwellers want to suggest with this the footprints of a vanished deity?

In Islam, a footprint (or its graphic interpretation) denotes the journey of the prophet Mohammed. In Tantrism it is the path of Vishnu, or the imprints of his hands, usually decorated

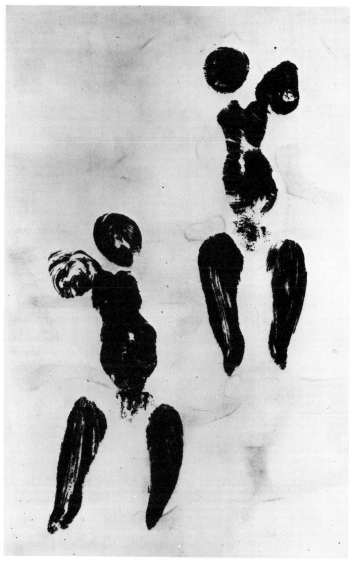

Fig 26
Yves Klein
Anthropométrie No. 132—1960.

with all kinds of symbols.

A woman in love presses the red of her lips on her love letters.

We know, of course, of fingerprints used as a signature, or a means of identification.

Since the Middle Ages, the idea of the shroud of St Veronica, supposedly imprinted with the features of Christ, has appealed to the imagination of the religious devotee.

The blue body-prints of women, which Yves Klein pro-

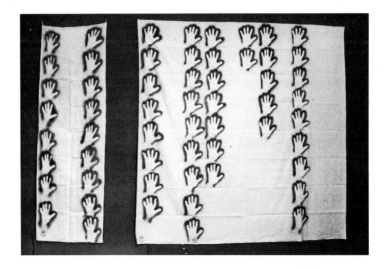

duced in 1960, mark an important stage in the history of the Zero art movement (fig. 26). Manzoni also developed a whole mythology around bodyprints. Nor can one forget the open-hand symbol (*La main ouverte*) of Le Corbusier (Bogotá and Chandigar, 1952). Around 1960 we find printed hands and faces in the work of Jasper Johns. Later we find all kinds of body-prints in the work of Arnulf Rainer and Hervé Fisher; the latter is renowned for his roller-towels stamped with hand-prints (*Art hygiénique*) (fig. 27). And *La Main Perdue* by Viallat has to be related to the 'empty' or negative hands of prehistory.

SCRIBBLES

I propose to deal with the scribble—the child's scribble in particular—before proceeding to graphics proper. It is the product of movement without meaning, and its only objective is *le plaisir de l'acte* (fig. 28). The scribble, executed with an instrument (pencil) and with the hand as driving force, is a futile action that precedes the conscious, significant, creative graphic. It is the chaos out of which the drawing develops. Or would we be right in saying that scribbling is already drawing? Rhoda Kellog, who has investigated more than 100,000 drawings of two- to four-year-olds, defines child scribbles according to 20 basic types (pointed, vertical, horizontal, diagonal, curved, zigzag ...). She goes on to show how combinations of these basic types evolve into primary archetypal figures (square, circle, triangle, St Andrew's cross, Greek cross). The commonest primary, structured, child drawing is the circle with the cross inside it. Arnheim in *Art and Visual Perception* writes:

To see organized form emerge in the scribbles of children is to watch one of the miracles of nature ... Circular shapes gradually appear in the clouds of zigzag strokes. At first they are rotations—traces of corresponding arm movements.

In the chaos of the scribble lies the trace of the sign. In the earliest child scribble the mechanical action is all-important yet even at this stage we can clearly distinguish drawing, the sign. The degree of spontaneity and movement in the scribble is already a manifestation of the personality of the child: there are weak, bold, soft, humble ... all kinds of scribbles. The scribble expresses something of the child and is already a message. Giorgio Celli writes in his preface to the catalogue *Origini dell' Arte* (Bologna, 1977):

Le tracce colorate antichissime di La Pasiega, i segni digitali de La Clotilde e di Gargas, non sono il preludio della pittura e dell' incisione; sono già incisione e pittura; come i grafismi dei bambini sono già non preludio di espressione, ma espressione.

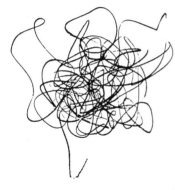

Fig 29
Paul Klee
Chaos

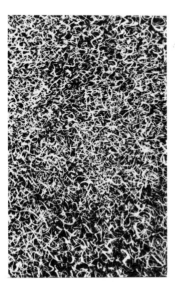

Fig 30
Mark Tobey
Toward the Whites—1957.

Not only in the world of the child, but also in psychiatric institutions, and on the walls of lavatories, as graffiti, we find these same, senseless scribbles.

The scribble, painted in lime, can also serve to make visible the windows of a new building. Sometimes, when on the telephone, the nervous man scribbles senselessly on a piece of paper lying in front of him.

Appealing through its minimal creative function and accidental character, the scribble is evident in the work of 20th-century artists such as Paul Klee (fig. 29), Cy Twombly, Mark Tobey (fig. 30), Peter Brüning, Fontana, Alechinsky, Fautrier, Hartung, Wols, Prillo, Jorn, Mathieu.

Klee, in his study *The Thinking Eye*, says that the chaos of the scribble becomes cosmic through the order brought to it by the coiled spiral. In the work of Twombly, scribbles have the charm of accident. In the canvases and drawings of Arshile Gorki, they are a nervous trait, running throughout the artist's work. The Cobra group used the scribble as an anti-representational, anti-aesthetic gesture of protest, as can be seen in the work of Appel, Alechinsky, and Jorn. The work of Wols and Dubuffet is full of nervous scribbles. With Fontana, scribbling becomes a refined sensual preoccupation. Georges Mathieu, following the precept that painting is a gestural action, produces works that suggest spattering fireworks or a type of calligraphy. These few but varied examples from the art of our own century attest to the usefulness of this graphic device, which at first sight may appear devoid of meaning.

We should now take a closer look at the child's scribble and at how this mindless action gradually develops into conscious drawing.

CHILD SCRIBBLES

A small child begins his first experiments with pencil and paper around the age that he learns to walk and develop a sense of balance. The first drawings are made purely for the pleasure of movement. This activity may even be charged with aggression. With the pencil clutched tightly in his fist, the child moves his whole arm vigorously, balancing this action with the rest of his body. The effect produced consists of straight or curving lines but is always drawn in one movement, without lifting the pencil.

At this stage the child is not particularly interested in his drawings. The result is of no importance: only the action counts. Yet when he discovers that his movements with pencil on paper leave behind a sign, he will start again, with renewed enthusiasm, this time because of the pleasure of the effect. He starts to experiment: isolated shapes come into existence on the page, because he lifts the pencil repeatedly in order to start anew. As the child's scribbles become more refined, we can distinguish a transition from continuous to

Fig 28.1
This drawing by Jan, 24 months old, is still a real scratch drawing with clear evidence of the importance of motor activity. Although we see certain structures like edges, coils, V-shapes, etc... we also see more controlled shapes like straight lines, curves and changes of direction amid the chaos.

Fig 28.2
A drawing by Inne, at 30 months, shows the influence on her of her surroundings and of the drawings of other children. There are deliberately-drawn circles, triangles and squares, as well as rhythmical zigzags and conscious groupings. The drawing is explained by the child in terms of: this is a flower . . . this is a house . . . this is mummy . . .

discontinuous lines: zigzags and loops appear in the drawing. The rhythm also slows down: the child acquires increasing control over his movements. New patterns of movement come into existence, no longer originating from the shoulder, as in the initial stage, but from the elbow and, finally, the wrist. Only now does the child begin to give meaning to his drawings: one scribble may represent his mother, another his dog.

At about the same time he discovers that the beginning and end of a line can meet each other and form a circle. He experiments endlessly with this new invention. Later on he discovers straight lines, which he will often practise for weeks before taking the next and final step, in giving meaning to all these forms. At last he is ready for figurative representations.

CHAPTER 2

PRIMAL SIGNS

DOTS/POINTS

The point is potential, fraught with possibilities. It is the All and the Nothing. The point—and, following on from it, the dot—is the beginning or birth, the visible manifestation of the immaterial point, the origin or starting point, the smallest graphic unit. The point itself is imaginary, indivisible, without dimension, space or form. René Guenon writes in his *Symbolisme de la Croix*: 'Le point, considéré en soi, n'est aucunement soumis a la condition spatiale, puisque, au contraire, il en est le principe'. Kandinsky, in *Punkt und Linie zu Flache*, says that the point is zero and silence, and that the time element is completely lacking. Tantrism says that the point is light itself beyond all colours, and therefore colourless. Extension of the point is impossible: anything larger is a little circle or a line. When manipulated, as, for example, in geometry, the point retains its fundamental qualities. When it becomes the centre of a radial structure, or of a circle, its nature does not change. From the moment we put a point in a space or on a surface, all other points (or elements) in that space or on that surface become related to that point, and each relation is unique.

Kandinsky (ibid.) maintains that the point is born the moment an implement (pin, pencil, pen...) touches the surface of a material.

Symbolically, the masculine point stands for the immovable centre, omphalos or axis of the entire world or cosmos; it represents fertility, the seed, sperm, out of which everything originates, the divine principle, simultaneously nothing and everything.

In certain primitive types of symbolism the point means ego. Following the anthropocentric principle: man stands at the centre of the Universe, the central factor in the cosmos. In this way, the macrocosm (with a divine presence or god at its centre) is reflected in the microcosm (with man at its centre).

●

Kandinsky/*Zero*
Also, in Tantrism, *The Last Tshakra.*

Opposite
Bronze-age petroglyph (Bohuslän, Sweden).
Sun-signs (concentric circles and a crossed circle) combine with anthropomorphic figures: warriors or sun-gods. Through the drawing runs a row of dots. Do these represent men?

45

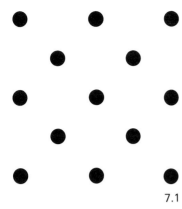

7.1

Although the point can mean birth, or the beginning, in Sufism it can equally well signify death, or the end to which everything returns (the reintegration in the divine).

Proclus (5th century A.D.) maintained that points have a cosmic power and rank in the first order among signs. Leibniz (1646–1716) drew a distinction between 'metaphysical points' and 'geometric points'.

Conventionally, we allow the point a minimal surface, so that it can be manipulated graphically, in symbolism and geometry (although it always retains its abstract, philosophical meaning).

Making dots with the fingers (dactylograms) belongs to the same series of physical, creative, primitive, sometimes rhythmical activities as handprinting. It is an autonomous activity, a rhythmical placing of points on body or object, using the fingertips.

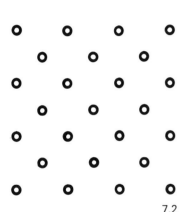

7.2

However, dots can also be made with instruments: a hollow, cylindrical stick (the cut stem of a reed) prints little open circles (7.2); a solid stick, little round spots or full circles (7.1). An instrument may be pressed into the clay of plates and dishes, or coated in pigment and stamped on to leather or fabrics. Or points may be made with a sharp instrument, as seen in rock walls in Malta.

The commonest way to form dots is nevertheless with the fingers. Toddlers (and sometimes adults) experience a primitive rhythmic pleasure when they are allowed to put dots on a white sheet with their fingers, or to print dots in the sand or on a steamed-up window pane.

Since prehistory, this has been a simple means of decoration and marking. We find points on the rock-faces of the Mousterian and early Aurignacian periods, and on the painted stones of the Mas d'Azil (France, 8000 B.C.) (7.3); on toys, coloured by children, in contemporary Mexico and Egypt; on

7.3

Point-drawings on the wall of a sanctuary in Kaba Kangaba, on the upper Nile (Mali, Africa).
The sanctuary was built by the Kita clan and dates from the 3rd-century B.C. Every seven years the clan restores the building. The point-drawings may be compared with prehistoric graphisms found on rock walls in Europe and America.

Fig 31
Yayoi Kusama
Self-obliteration—1968.

the earthenware of the early Cretans and present-day African primitives; and in the drawings of Paul Klee and Juan Miró. They also appear in the erotic-sexual obsessions of Yayoy Kusama who covered people and environments in coloured dots, as part of a magical, playful, group-sex ritual (fig. 31).

The dot or point is an important element in the work of a number of 20th-century artists: Mavignier, Fontana, Gonchior (fig. 32), Uecker, Bury, Larry Poons, Scaccabarozzi....

Fig 32
Küno Gonchior
Drawing

The point is that which is indivisible.
Euclid—*Elements*.

In the Korean *han'gul* writing, alphabetized in 1443, the symbol ● (phonetically *a*) means 'heaven', but this sign is also related to ○, which was originally the symbol for 'throat'.

In Hebrew, the point means the origin (*Shekinah*).

The Cabbala calls the point the first *sephira* (divine emanation) or the first *kether*. According to the Zohar, the Hidden Spirit originally produced a single point, which was converted into thought.

Fig 33
Wall-painting of Bison.
Cave at Marsoulas, France.

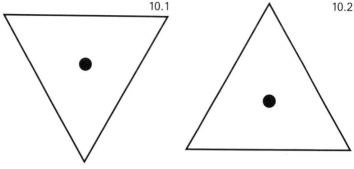

10.1

10.2

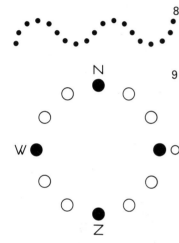

8

9

N

W

Z

In Tantrism, *bindu* (point) means the most extreme concentration of energy, beyond which it is impossible to go: nothing can be condensed any further. When this point becomes a centre, out of which the environment is determined, it is called *mahabindu*, or the big point.

For the Arapaho Indians, the point means man. Many points signify a number of people or warriors.

Dots are the primeval form of glyphs (notches); they may be used as a type of filling for a drawing (fig. 33), or become a compositional element of the drawing itself (8). It is possible that primeval circle drawings were first laid out with little stones or seeds (points) and were subsequently imitated graphically. The compass may have originated in the same way (9): the first four stones were laid out, indicating the four main points or directions, then further stones were added for the intermediate points.

In Tantrism, the point means seed or sperm when it is placed in an inverted triangle or in the centre of a diamond (10.1). In a triangle with the point upwards, the point means the 'eye of God' (10.2).

Placed in a square or diamond, the point can give these forms a totally new meaning.

SCRATCHES
FROM SCRATCH TO LINE

The scratch is another basic primal sign, a starting point for various motifs and decorations. But, unlike the point or dot, it may also count as a real graphic device. The scratch can be made on a surface with the fingernails, or with a pin, through a movement of the hand alone. It marks an important cultural step forward in the evolution of the sign: it is drawing (fig. 34). The simple scratch may signify destruction, violation, death or aggression; it may be used as a means of marking property; or it may suggest the vulva or penis—but then usually with strong emotional overtones. The scratch *marks*. The scratch manifests human presence: *I am*.

As for the device itself, one can draw a distinction between the straight scratch (11, a.b.c.), usually thicker at the beginning (above) and thinner at the end (below) (in other words, wedge-shaped) and the curved scratch (12, a.b.) which follows a circular movement of the hand. Scratches are usually made to the left (11, a.) (12, a.) or the right (11, b.) (12, b.); they are rarely made vertically, unless by a conscious effort and intentional act (11, c.).

The scratch has enormous graphic potential, and has been used by artists from antiquity up to the present day. Scratches slanted to the right or left or arranged in vertical sequence (13, a.b.c.)* often symbolize rain, while the single straight scratch may suggest the vulva or the penis (11, c.); in all cases these are therefore fertility symbols.

Curved scratches (13, d.e.f.) produced by circular movements of the hand** may lie at the origin of a prehistoric

Fig 34
Frankish vase or pot, decorated with scratches. Royal Museum of Art and History, Brussels.

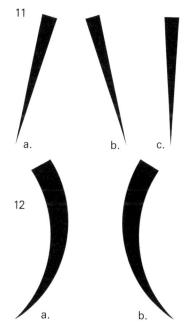

11

a.   b.   c.

12

a.   b.

---

*Strokes sloping to the right (/) have, in Chinese writing, an active meaning (*biè* or *piè*=active movement). Strokes sloping to the left (\) mean passivity (*fú*=weakness). Left and right sloping lines crossing to form X (*yì*) mean to reign, to rule, to lead, to correct, to regulate ... If they join to form an inverted fork (∧) this suggests the idea of dividing or separating.
**The arm can have three arcs, each centred or pivoted on a different joint: the wrist, the elbow and the shoulder.

13   a.   b.   c.

      d.   e.   f.

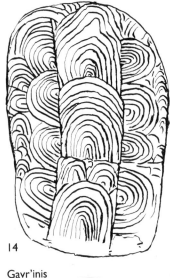

14

Gavr'inis

composition made up of semicircles or 'bows' (14), Gavr'inis, Le Morbihan, France; Slieve-na-Calliagh, County Meath, Ireland; La Zarza, Canary Islands. Such compositions are often interpreted as labyrinths, but have also been associated with the rising and setting sun. The bow pattern is graphically interesting because, radiating from the centre point, it develops itself rhythmically from small to large.

The double bow often refers to female fertility (Cameroon).

Is the scratch really the primal form or origin of the rational, consciously-drawn straight line (15, d.), as in the connection between two points (15, a.) or, radiating from the point, a continuation line of indeterminate length (15, b.)? At this stage it would seem inevitable that the primitive graphic artist would discover the cross, if not the + (vertical/horizontal) (16, a.) then at least the × (diagonal) (16, b.). But in fact nothing is farther from the truth. Hundreds of years may elapse before this combination is reached. Thus the cross was unknown in Asia Minor for centuries, until the Cretans imported it. J. C. Bédard, in *Pour Un Art Schématique* even maintains:

La croix a été produite à un moment difficilement situable dans l'ordre d'apparition des signes (op. cit., page 108).

One could illustrate with countless examples of 20th-century art just how expressive the scratch may be: consider the works of Klee, Fontana, Twombly, Brüning, Tapies...

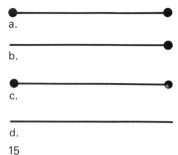

a.

b.

c.

d.

15

16

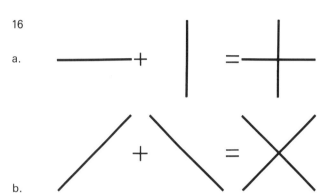

a.

b.

Fig 35
Building in Nigeria decorated with curved, bow-shaped designs. Compare these with the similar, rhythmic designs on stones found at Gavr'inis (14, opposite).

SCRATCH STRUCTURES

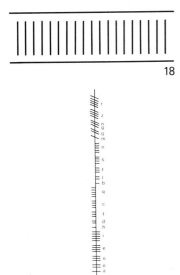

18

Fig 36
Ogham alphabet, from pre-Christian Ireland.
A primitive writing system that was probably related to notched sticks that were used in much greater antiquity.

19

With the scratch, many graphic combinations can come into existence. In the earliest cultural stages, scratch motifs may appear chaotic, yet hints of patterns already show through them, which will later become more apparent. The first and oldest scratch drawings consist of series of notches (18)...these can be found just about everywhere and date from the Mousterian and Chattelperonian periods. Despite their rhythmical arrangement, they are difficult to interpret. Are they some kind of scoreboard? A calendar? A simplified game? According to Leroi-Gourhan, these are the oldest graphic compositions of *Homo sapiens*, dating from between the 35th and 20th millennia. In his attempt at interpretation, Leroi-Gourhan compares them to the Churinga drawings found in Australia, which also show an attempt to be rhythmical. These latter consist of concentric point drawings, made by the finger of the officiant during ritual ceremonies, following the rhythm of his declamation: the graphic rhythm follows the verbal one. Other writers have seen a relationship with fertility symbolism. Possible parallels may also be drawn with the pre-Christian Celtic ogham alphabet (fig. 36).

In combining the right-slanting scratch with the left-slanting scratch, the V or wedge originates (19), a distinct and explicit vulval symbol (also suggesting the tip of an arrow or knife, a bird, wound, cut or cleft ... but also up and down, in and out).

V-shapes are possible components of all sorts of crosses (19). They also appear frequently, horizontally or vertically, in all primitive cultures. When they are placed side by side they can even create zigzags (20). One stone at Gavr'inis (Le Morbihan, France) shows the transition from a to b, as a join is made between two diagonals. The final step is taken when a continuous zigzag is formed, first horizontally (20, c.), then vertically (21). When two V-shapes are placed on top of each other (22), they form a diamond (vagina/astral sign), also found at Gavr'inis.

52

The 90° angle, although it has totally different qualities, is definitely related to the V-shape or wedge. It is also associated with the cross, and can develop out of a halving of the cross (23, a.) The way in which it is made is significant in the development of primitive sign vocabulary: the draughtsman draws the vertical line and suddenly changes direction—to the left or right; he draws a horizontal line and at a certain moment changes direction—up or down. The 90° angle has the same radical qualities as the cross: it is constructive, graphically strong, rational, functional.... With four right-angles one can construct a square. The right-angle (gamma) is also a component of the gammadion, the swastika, and its variants (see pages 78–79).

The Greek tau-cross or T-cross (*crux commissa*) (23, b.c.d.e.), also called the cross of St Anthony, is related to the hammer of Thor and the *crux simplex* (cross minus one arm). With the addition of a loop, the tau-cross becomes the Egyptian ankh-cross or *crux ansata* (cross with handle), a symbol of life (23, f.).

We find the same sign in hieroglyphic and linear Cretan script. Later it is used as a Christian symbol. It is likely that the T-cross originated from the simple conjunction of vertical and horizontal lines. In the case of 23, b., we read the conjunction of man (vertical) and woman (horizontal); man (v) and earth (h); active (v) and passive (h); tree (v) and ground (h). In 23, d., we see an androgynous sign as well as a tectiform sign, a hammer and an axe. The T-sign makes a strong visual

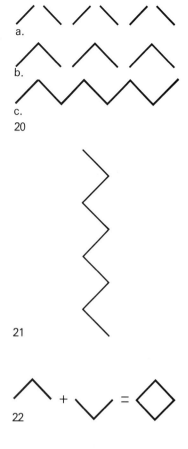

a.

b.

c.

20

21

22

23.a

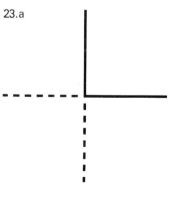

Wall design from Fez (Morocco)

53

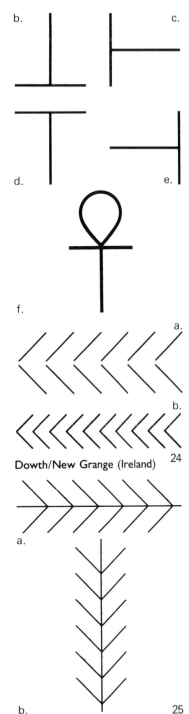

b.

c.

d.

e.

f.

a.

b.

Dowth/New Grange (Ireland) 24

a.

b. 25

impression in each of its four variants.

One of the commonest patterns composed of scratches is the fish-bone. It can originate freely and rhythmically (24, a.b.) sometimes combining scratches (24, a.) or chevrons (24, b.), or it may be a more conscious imitation of a fish-bone or feather (25, a.b.). Acording to Leroi-Gourhan, the feather can symbolize a phallus. Vertically, it resembles a plant or tree (25, b.). In areas where the palm tree grows, this is the tree that is generally imitated. In other areas the fern or pine may be the source of inspiration. In prehistory, this graphic device is sometimes used (Niaux-La Vache, France) as an ithyphallic sign (A. Leroi-Gourhan).* A three-dimensional effect may be added by positive-negative colouring, as in wickerwork (26, a.b.) . Yet surely the simple graphic pattern is more appealing, originating as it does out of a pure sense of rhythm, although perhaps subconsciously influenced by elements such as fish-bones, trees, plants and fossils....

Just as fish-bone patterns may have originated in the pleasure of drawing a counter-rhythm, left to right, up and down, it may be that certain cross-structures developed according to the same principle: a rhythmic structure with right-slanting scratches (27, a.) superimposed on a structure with scratches slanting to the left (27, b.). Combinations of series could follow on from this, eventually crossed by horizontal lines (29, a.b.). In this way, diamonds and triangles are formed, becoming more distinct if executed positively–negatively (30).

Another pattern of triangular structures comes into existence by connecting all points of intersection (30). Possibly a primitive designer could develop the square and the triangle from such structures.

The scratch makes us think of the works of Fontana, in which it sometimes became a notch or tear, or of the beautiful shadings of Agnes Martin, or of the obsessional drawings of Jan Schoonhoven, to mention only a few.

---

*These phallic symbols often appear associated with animals, especially with animals that lick each other (bear or deer), which in conjunction may be interpreted as a fertility ritual. Rhomboidal (vulval) signs often appear in a similar context.

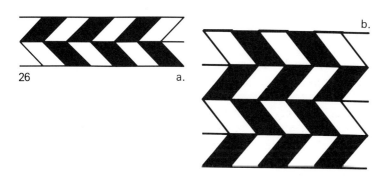

26   a.

b.

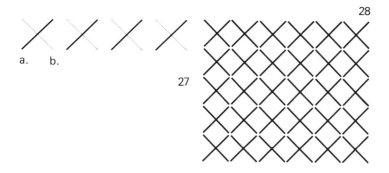

28

a.   b.

27

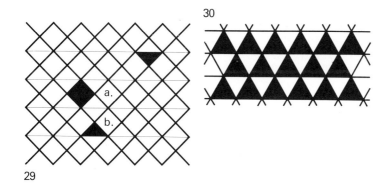

30

a.

b.

29

55

WAVY AND ZIGZAG LINES

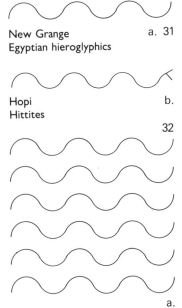

New Grange   a. 31
Egyptian hieroglyphics

Hopi   b.
Hittites

                  32

                  a.

Knowth (County Meath, Ireland)
Ashanti (Abampruwa Adakawa)

Together with the dot (or point) and the scratch, the wavy line (undulating, serpentine, sinusoidal) (31, a.), which is more primitive than the straight line, appears as one of man's earliest, most primal graphic marks. The single wavy line is readily associated with the snake (the chthonic, the divine, the diabolic, the sexual, the solar, the powerful, the living line...) (31, b.) or with the track left by the snake or sometimes also with the movement of a whip. In Judeo-Christian culture the snake is charged with deeper symbolism: that of negative sexuality.

A pattern of five wavy lines, drawn with the five fingers spread out, the product of a waving movement, is found in even the oldest cultures. This sign, drawn into a soft surface such as sand, automatically and universally symbolizes the wave movement of water; it is also a fertility symbol. Usually the five lines run horizontally in parallel (32, a.). Sometimes a positive–negative alternation is created by the use of dots (32, b.), scratches (32, c.) or shading (32, d.) between the lines. This combines different basic graphic techniques, incorporating dots or scratches as rhythmic graphic elements.

b.   c.   d.

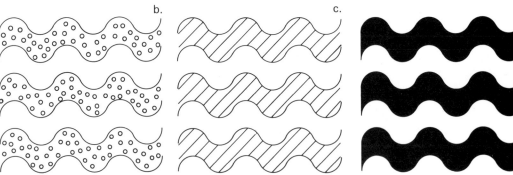

The first derivative of the elegant, spontaneously-drawn wavy line is the angular, deliberately-drawn zigzag line (33), recognized as the symbol for mountains in having an ascending/descending rhythm, and also for fire. The Hittite ideogram (34) (with 3 points—the same as in Old Chinese bone-writing) means parapet, or wall of a fortress. The zigzag line likewise represents in many cultures a snake (made clear by the addition of a head), often used as a magical sign (33, b.). To the Hopi Indians it means lightning. For other Indian tribes it is the mark of the bat.

Jean Paul Barbier (*Symbolique et Motifs du Sud de Nias*) found that the zigzag line (*dent de scie*) is found all over Indonesia, as also is the wavy line. He links them with the plaited image of two intertwined snakes. It is interesting to compare this with the snake motif of the Ur period (Mesopotamia—first dynasty), in which it was the symbol of fertility and the eternal recreation of life (34, I.). In a further stage of development the combination of the snake and staff (trunk or column) is found, which results in the *caduceus* (34, 2.), whose many variations and interpretations reflect its enormous symbolic and cosmic significance.

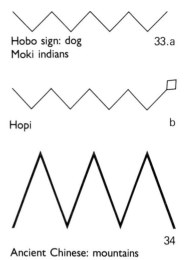

Hobo sign: dog — 33.a
Moki indians

Hopi — b

Ancient Chinese: mountains — 34

Ur — 34.1

34.2

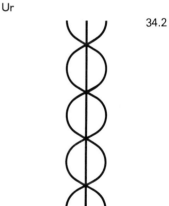

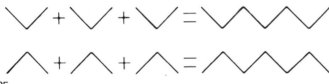

35

There are also authors who maintain that the zigzag line is a linking together of the V (or wedge) (see page 52), or of the A (alpha) (35).

Again, structural formations and positive–negative shading-in occurs (36, a.b.).

a.   b.   36

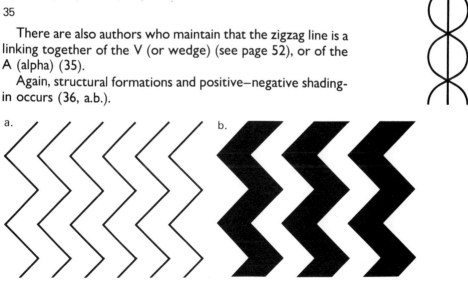

Egyptian hieroglyph.
New Grange, Ireland.

37

38

39

In Egyptian hieroglyphics, three zigzag lines placed above one another mean water: specifically, river water (37).

At a later stage of cultural development can be found rectangular ascending and descending movements—once again, a stylized form of the wavy line (38).

Analogous to combined zigzag lines is the pattern obtained by joining crosses (see page 55) either vertically or horizontally (41). On a capstone from New Grange, Ireland, there is a double zigzag with a series of joined diamonds (39) immediately below it; the latter are obviously a variation on the simpler drawing above them. It may be concluded from this that diamonds and therefore also squares often originated from the superimposition of zigzag drawings. In Fourknocks, County Meath, Ireland, zigzag markings face each other: one set is an inversion of the other, with diamond shapes drawn between the two (40).

Superimposed wavy lines (42) often appear in primitive decoration, but are neither coloured nor shaded in positive—negative form. Sometimes they are drawn vertically (43, a.b.) (Gavr'inis, France).

Double-wavy and double-zigzag lines often represent the double snake (e.g., the *caduceus*) while simultaneously symbolizing complementary unity in a yin-yang sense.

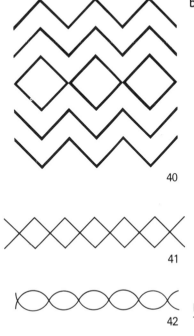

40

41

42

a.   b.   43

Moki   New Mexico
Thebes

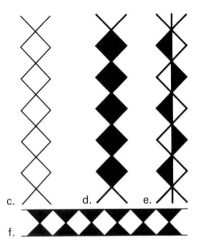

c.   d.   e.

f.

STRAIGHT LINES: FROM THE HORIZONTAL AND VERTICAL TO THE CROSS

Is the straight line simply an extension, a rationalization of the scratch? Or is it really a joining-up of equidistant points, but perceived primarily as a straight line? Or is the straight line a product of the point-in-motion?

It has earlier been argued that the point is imaginary, lacking both surface and dimension. If so, how can a joining-up of points result in a line? How, that is, unless all the point's metaphysical aspects are ignored and it is given a conventional physical dimension? But here we start getting into a geometrical, graphical game...

What is certain is that the evolution of the playful, wavy line predates that of the purposeful, straight line, and that the straight line already presupposes some form of reasoned correction—a form of censorship, in fact—in being a conscious, controlled graphic act.

Thus the flowing handwritten Chinese figure I (one) (45, a.) retains the fluency of the waving hand-movement, whereas adapted into a stylized form it becomes tensely horizontal (45, b.). The straight line can symbolize a tight cord or bow-string. When it lacks either beginning or end but is infinitely long in both directions; when it starts from one point and extends indefinitely in one direction; or when it simply joins two points: in any such form it ranks among man's primary geometrical obsessions, an important technical stage in the process of becoming civilized.

A straight vertical line can divide a surface into left and right (46, a.); a straight horizontal one can divide it into above and below (46, b.). Thus as well as having intrinsic graphic quality the straight line has the capacity to act *upon* space, and upon the surface on which it appears. It divides; it creates order; it is radical and unambiguous.

The horizontal line (46, b.) (running parallel with the horizon, possibly?) would be classed as feminine/passive, in contrast to the masculine/active vertical line (46, a.) (parallel

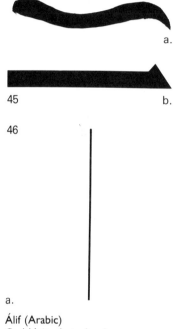

45   a.

45   b.

46

a.

Álif (Arabic)
God-Unity (astrology)
Inuit (Kiatéxamut indians): human being/man/active.

b.

Earth (astrology)
Blackfoot indians: human being/ dead person/woman/passive.

METARON

אלה (ELEH)

מי (MI)

SAMAEL   (ELOHIM)

אֱלֹהִים

= TELĖSMA

47

48
a.

1   2   3   4   5

b.

4

3

2

1

Valcamonica (Italy)   49

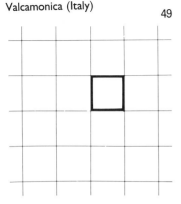

to the upright man). The vertical line symbolizes the axis, the pivot, man, 'the tree of the world', and also the phallus, the spear, the sceptre, the column. It is symbolic too of life, health, growth and, simultaneously, of stability and activity. The plummeting vertical line symbolizes also the staff: the power, meaning '*isi*'—'demand'—in runic script.

The vertical line is always a reminder of the connection between above and below, between heaven and earth, between spirit and matter; the androgynous man with his head in the cosmos and his feet on the earth. It is the axis, the centre of time and space.

The horizontal line (46, b.), passive and static, divides a whole series of opposites: above/below, heaven/earth, air/ land, light/dark, good/bad, heaven/hell, yin/yang . . .

In the Cabbala, the horizontal line symbolizes the division between above (*eleh*) and below (*mi*)—the universal principle (*telesma*) (47). Elsewhere, the Cabbala says: 'What is above is equal to what is below, and what is below is equal to what is above': the Cabbalistic inversion. In the Korean *han'gul* script, the horizontal — (phonetically, *u*) is derived from the same ideographic image that symbolizes 'earth', and the vertical | (phonetically, *i*) means 'man'.

The line is length without width. The ends of a line are points.
The straight line is also that which joins two points.
Euclid—*Elements*

The next obvious step is the rhythmic repetition of the horizontal and vertical lines. According to Klee, the sequence is 1, 2, 3, 4, 5, left to right, bottom to top (48, a.b.). The horizontal–vertical combination follows naturally: the chequerboard, with its strong optical effect, from which may

50   Valcamonica (Italy)   51   Greek vase

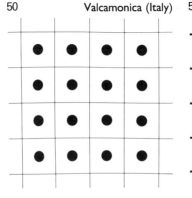

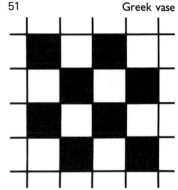

come the square (49). Sometimes the pattern is filled in with dots (50). At other times it is shaded in (51), often symbolizing day/night, light/dark, good/bad: an apt illustration of opposites (compare with yin-yang), still seen today in the symbols of religion and Freemasonry, and in air-traffic signalling, racing or heraldry.

In Egyptian hieroglyphics, the chequerboard (52) means 'house'. The squares represent the rooms.

When a vertical line is superimposed squarely upon a horizontal one, the Greek cross, *crux simplex*, appears (53); when rotated diagonally, the variant cross of St Andrew, *crux decussata* (54), is formed (see also page 51).

The equilateral cross can be seen to originate from a geographical N:S/E:W orientation (55, a.b.). It can also be formed from the simple act of placing two small bars across each other (runes), or through more complex combinations, such as those in diagrams 56, 57 and 58.

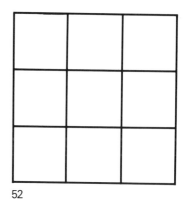
52

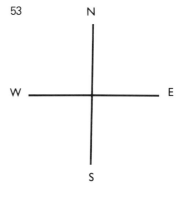
53

54

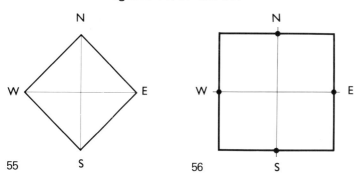

55

56

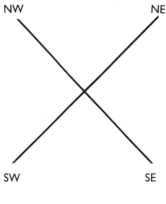

The square can be produced by the simple action of joining the points of a cross (55).

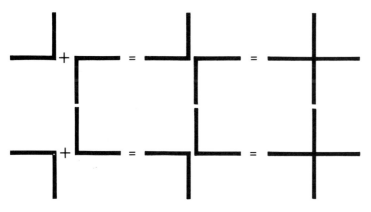

61

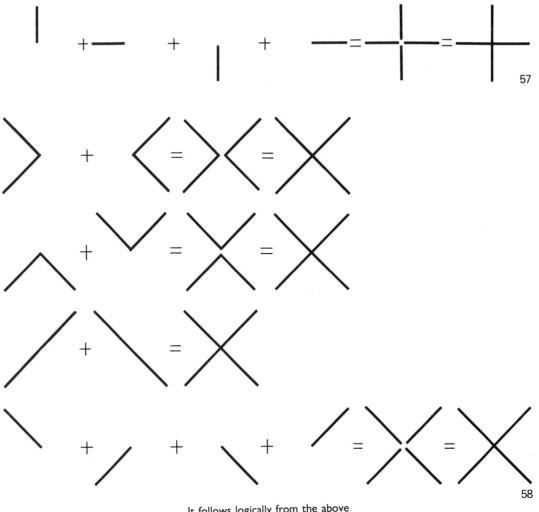

57

58

It follows logically from the above that:

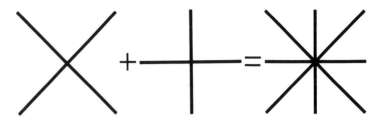

62

SPIRALS
CONCENTRIC CIRCLES
CONCENTRIC SQUARES
CONCENTRIC TRIANGLES

The macrocosmic spiral or vortex (59) most certainly predates the circle. A complete self-contained system and, again, an archetypal primal form, it has its origins in spontaneous, mechanical hand-movements. As an iconographic mark it has been ever-present since the dawn of history.

The central point of a spiral—its beginning or its end—can represent tranquillity, stillness, timelessness, equilibrium, release, stability; it symbolizes the navel and the axis. This simple motif—nothing more than a coiled line—can be connected in the imagination with the moon, the sun, the vulva (signifying fertility), indeed with everything that evokes the evolving cycle of time.

The spiral, in contrast to the endless circle, moves towards and ends at the centre. Different civilizations associate it not only with the snake, the snail, the whirlwind or whirlpool, but also with the curly tails of monkeys, dogs or cats, or with human curly hair, whether pubic, facial or on the head.

As a primal sign, it is obvious that the spiral is closely related to the wavy line. Not only do both derive from mechanical hand-movements, but both are also used frequently to represent the snake-form: that is, the moving and the coiled line. The Navajo Indians in particular use the image of a spiral snake as a magical and religious symbol, often in sand-drawings (fig. 17, page 28). Among the South American Huichol Indians, the spiral refers to the watersnake, Tatei Narihuane: Our Mother the Rain Messenger.

Square spirals are also found in the vast earth-drawings of Nazca.

In the Cabbala, the Hebrew letter Yod in the Tetragrammaton* stands for the symbol of the coiled, passive snake, representing the potency of creativity. The snake motif is also linked to the spiral (and vice versa) in prehistoric Celtic,

59

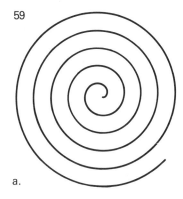

a.

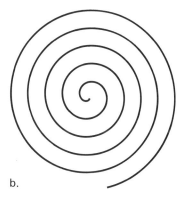

b.

Bugibba
Hagar Qim
Hittites
Thrace
New Grange

---

*Tetragrammaton, or Tetragram: a word based on four consonants.

63

Fig 38
Octopus

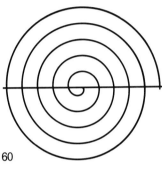

60

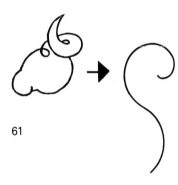

61

Indian, Pre-Columbian and African civilizations. And the snake itself is for many civilizations the symbol of wisdom and eternity.

In the Mediterranean region, the cuttlefish or octopus is a similar inspiration, its waving tentacles, drawn again and again, sometimes inducing abstract spirals.

The sun-spiral, rotating clockwise (59, a.), is sometimes known as the creative or positive spiral: a reference to Pallas Athene. By way of contrast, the moon-spiral, turning anti-clockwise, whirlwind-fashion (59, b.), is called destructive or negative, in reference to Poseidon.

In *Die Sonne als Symbol*, Rudolf Engler argues that the origin of the spiral as a symbol for the solstice lies in its similarity to a continuously rising sun: in support he offers a remarkable diagram (60).

The spiral character in Hittite script (phonetically, *ma*) is derived from the ram's horns (61).

In the earliest stages of Chinese bone-writing, an oscillating spiral is used as a pictogram for sun/day/light (62). Subsequently replaced by two concentric circles (62, 1.), it emerges finally as a circle around a point (62, 2.).*

The next, still archaic, form is a circle bisected horizontally (62, 3.), which evolves first into an eye-like form (62, 4.) and then into a horizontally bisected square (62, 5.), which in its modern Kai Ssu Chinese form (63) is pronounced phonetically *ya*. This would seem to support my emphatic belief that the cosmic spiral is the primary form both of concentric circles and of the circle itself.

---

*Evidently a development of this is the double sign of a square (6), which carries the meaning or signification 'time': 'At one time', or: 'Once', as well as the spatial instruction: 'Surround, circumscribe' (see also page 104).

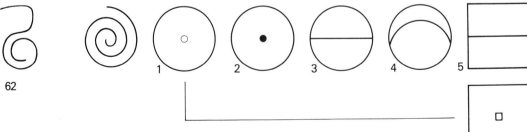

62

1   2   3   4   5

Possibly in some cultures the spiral form evolved neither from natural spiralling hand-movements nor from any spiral forms found in nature, such as snails, coiled snakes, ram's horns or whirlpools, but emerged at a later stage, inspired by designs observed on the spiral-plaited bottoms of baskets, or the clay-coiled bottoms of jars.

The spiral, with its powerfully cosmic overtones, symbolizes time, the span of life. A spiral that rotates towards and ends at the centre signifies death and destruction; one that rotates away from the centre signifies birth. An infinitely growing spiral represents the ideas of birth, growth, resurrection, rebirth and procreation.

The double spiral, as well as the spiral returning into itself (64), and the reversed double spiral (65 and 66), represent the union of opposites: life and death, vitality and destructiveness, yin and yang (67). Evident in both the returning and the reversed forms is the symbol of rebirth: entering the womb of Mother Earth so as to be later reborn. In the reversed spiral (65 and 66), the flow of energy from one side to the other is very clear.

In the East, the double spiral (*oculi*: breast-like) appears by the time of the Dongson period (the Indonesian bronze-age), just before the beginning of our era. Found first on steles and earrings, the symbol is used later on in reference to a bull's horns, but originally symbolized the concept of duality—destruction-and-renewal, referring to the cult of the snake, to nature's continuous renewal, and having a clear parallel in the cult of Shiva (J. P. Barbier).

Similarly, in the Churinga cult of central Australia (fig. 39), as in many others, concentric circles (69) are bound up with the notions of birth and rebirth, growth, and the evolution of the cosmos.

63

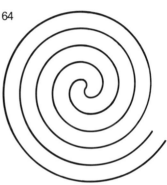

64

Oued Djerat, Tassili, Algeria
Maori Moko-moko heads, New Zealand

65

Maya

66

Newgrange
Etruscan

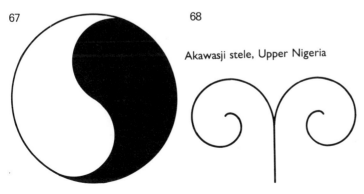

67

68

Akawasji stele, Upper Nigeria

Fig 39
Churinga ritual with aborigines of central Australia.

Churingas/Chirungas (Australia)
Loughcrew/Knowth/Newgrange
(Ireland)   69

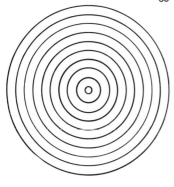

Fig 40
Mandala

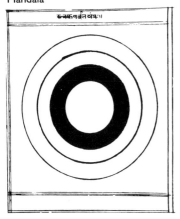

There are also concentric mandalas and yantras: Indian and Tibetan geometric devotional drawings, with all their multiple variants. More than simply intense visual images, they are essentially sacred forms used as an aid in meditation (fig. 40). For the new convert to the Tantric religion, the mandala simultaneously gives protection against the outside world and guides him towards, helps him to focus on, the heart of things, the *I*, the sacred, the centre of the cosmos. And not only in the East but in the West too, in Christianity, the concentric circle (fig. 41) has a clear religious function. Such concentric forms are also found in central Africa (in the Ashanti, Ghana, and Dogon cultures).

All over the world, concentric circles are used in carving primitive masks, to represent the eyes and intensify the impression of looking (Bobo mask, fig. 13; Baineng mask, fig. 42).

The relationship between the spiral and the labyrinth is also evident. (*Labrys* means double axe, referring also to the double-axe sign.) The labyrinth at Knossos was a game that was safe only for the initiated. Only they were able to survive the journey to the deadly centre and then embark on the return journey towards rebirth. It was a fatally confusing game, one in which evil spirits also became entangled.

The labyrinth is a universal, durable product of the human imagination, and has hundreds of interpretations. In its Christianized form, *The Road to Jerusalem*, it is Christ, representing salvation, who is the centre. In Islam, the Kufic form denoting labyrinthine meandering is the writing used for the name of Mohammed (fig. 44). From the earliest Celtic and Scandinavian cultures to the rock drawings of Valcamonica, through the Babylonian, Mycenaean and Ancient Greek civilizations, to the present day, this looping umbilical-cord symbol retains its potency for man.

Freud referred to the labyrinth as the 'anal birth'. Certainly it alludes to man's difficult path through life, which leads either to his destruction (death/hell) or to his salvation (heaven).

Some writers link the labyrinth with the swastika and with bow-drawings, such as those of Gavr'inis (Brittany).

The first variation on the spiral is the square spiral (70, a.b.), from which concentric squares (71) may subsequently be derived. But unlike concentric circles, it is not so clear that concentric squares were derived from the square spiral.

Less obvious variations, and therefore also less common, are triangular spirals (72, a.b.) and concentric triangles (73). The latter, however, are applied frequently in mantras and yantras.

There are many derivations from the spiral: the double spiral (65), the chain spiral (74), spirals that reverse and face each other (75), the swastika spiral (76 and 77). Indeed, spirals, whether stamped on pastry, or used in fashion or on jewellery, are among the most common decorations.

Fig 41
Map of heaven. 14th-century French miniature.
Bibliothèque Nationale, Paris.

Ashanti gold-weight

Fig 42
Baineng mask from the Barbier–Müller collection (Geneva). Concentric circles around the eyes reinforce their impact.

67

Fig 44
Kufic calligraphy in the form of a labyrinth, based on the writing of the name of Mohammed. See also a calligraphic labyrinth based on the name of Ali, p.123.

Fig 45
The primary relation between spirals and concentric circles is evident in these labyrinthine pattens on rock walls at Mongor, Spain.

Fig 43
The Christ on this ivory reliquary from the Frankish period (750 A.D.) is an example from our Western civilization of concentric circles being used to reinforce the impact of the eyes.

70   a.   b.

Maya (Uxmal, Mexico)
Zapotec (Mitla, Mexico)

71

Cretan (Greece)
Mixtec (Mexico)

72   Anasazi indians   a.   b.

73   Ashanti

74

Tarquinia/Apulia (Italy)

75

76   Crete

77

69

THE CROSS
THE DOUBLE AXE
THE SWASTIKA

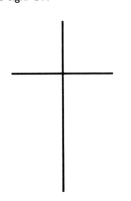

78

Hallstadt
Assyria
Hobo sign: OK

79

Crux imissa (latin)
Chou (Chinese)/To (Japanese) = 10

The origins of the cross-form (*crux quadrata, crux simplex*) (78) are to be found in the combination of a vertical and a horizontal line (spirit and matter), or in the NE–SW/NW–SE formation. It may refer to time and the seasons of the year, or symbolically to vertical man, arms outstretched, androgynous and utterly static—as, obviously, in the case of the Latin cross. In Islam, it symbolizes universal man, while for the Assyrians, Hindus, Celts and Greeks it signifies a tree (the tree of life, indeed) or the sun.

The cross has always been the quaternary, dynamic symbol of order and harmony: in man, in life itself, and in nature and the cosmos. It represents the four stages of man's life, the four points of the compass, the four moments of the day, the four seasons, the four phases of the moon—the creation of structural order out of chaos.

The cross divides a surface decisively into four parts, making a strong visual impact which is often experienced as a violation of that surface. So it is little wonder that the cross positively *demands* attention, and that the significance of the action is impossible to ignore. For the cross, the anti-chaos, imparts a structure to a surface or space, ordering itself not only by indicating directions (NS–EW) but also by outlining four separate individual spaces, each of which may acquire an autonomous function. The right-angle (90°) originates at the point of intersection of the vertical and horizontal lines, and is thus significant in all civilizations, because of its practical and constructive qualities in particular.

That point in the cross where the horizontal and vertical lines intersect is important—the *I* (centre o, the cosmos), where the heavenly and earthly meet; the Godhead and divinity; the union of opposites: masculine and feminine, positive and negative, life and death, the active and passive principles.

For the Mayas, the cross meant the cosmic division of the

70

compass into four points, or continents, with the fifth continent as the centre. In the Egyptian hieroglyphic script, the cross symbolizes destruction and revenge, whereas the tau-cross (St Anthony's cross) means life and the tree of life, the phallus, the symbol of fertility.

The centre of the Islamic compass is called the Kaaba: one corner of the veil that covers the holy stone coincides with the east side, and is known as the 'black angle'; the other angles bear the names of Yemen (South), Iraq (North) and Syria (West). The Muslims draw the north to point towards the bottom of a map or drawing (81).

For the Dakota Indians, the Greek cross is the anthropomorphic image of orientation. The top of the cross points in the direction of the north wind—the most cold and powerful—but at the same time it is associated with the head, the seat of intelligence. The left arm, pointing in the direction of the east wind, is associated with the heart, the home of life and love. The foot of the cross points towards the burning south wind, and is the seat of ardent passion. The right arm, in the direction of the friendly west wind, relates to the lungs, from which breath ultimately escapes softly into the unknown night. The centre of the cross, the point of intersection, locates the earth, where man is cast into the battle raging between the gods and the winds.

The intersection of the vertical and the horizontal is the Holy Palace of the Cabbala. In many other symbolic systems, this point is the place where the contraries are anihilated. This is the point of zero, rest, harmony, order, equilibrium. Many primitives are obsessed by this fifth point and separate it from the four arms of the cross. By doing this they recognize the special meaning of the point: the centre of the system, of the macrocosm, or of the microcosm (82).

In writing about this fifth point, the point of intersection, M. Seuphor declares: 'Un point crucial en vérité ... est toute chose, autant le oui que le non, l'être et le non-être.'

Yet, by contrast, the symbol does not have such profound significance: for many North American Indians the cross simply carries the meaning of 'star'; for the Eskimos, a cross-pattern represents a flight of birds; while elsewhere the cross is simply the sign of the tribe (the Cheyenne, for example).

In death-symbolism, the cross means the victory of life over death: the woman, the horizontal line, receives the man, the vertical line. In Christianity, too, the death of Christ on the cross acquires the meaning of the victory of life over death,

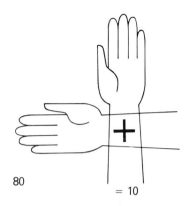

80

= 10

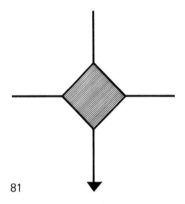

81

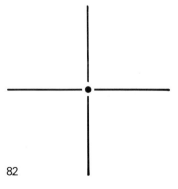

82

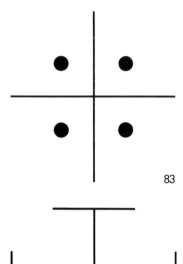

83

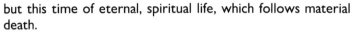

84

Holy Roman Empire (12th-century).

85

but this time of eternal, spiritual life, which follows material death.

The cross, being a quaternary symbol, is somtimes augmented by placing four points in the corners, an enhancement that is also found in the Cabbalistic symbol of the Rosicrucians (83). The cross of Jerusalem also has this clear quaternary reference, and, moreover, a reference to its possible origin, namely the cross-in-a-square. This sign was already used in the Tell Halaf civilization (Mesopotamia, 5th millennium B.C.) (84). In prehistory, however, crosses were tectiforms, or solar cosmic signs.

Jung claims that the vertical–horizontal cross (78) is a spiritually neutral symbol, in contrast to the cross of St Andrew (85), which is dynamic and spiritually active.
In runic script, the cross of St Andrew has the meaning of 'giving' (*geba*), which means also 'gift'. And from the earliest humanity to the present day it is possible to recognize in this rotating cross that point where roads or paths intersect: a crossroads, in other words.

Already, in its primitive form, the cross, powerfully cosmic and astral, is both centrifugal (86, a.) and centripetal (86, b.). This duality survives through its later developments. For example, as the symbol used by the first Christians, it refers simultaneously to death and resurrection, to destruction and salvation.* For instance, in the altarstone of Mont St-Michel at Carnac, France (87) there are forms of crosses in which the centripetal force is clearly drawn and reinforced by arrows. But in a Sioux-Indian image in the Museum of the American Indians in New York, not only is the centre accentuated, but the centrifugal force of the cross-sign is also emphasized (88). Compare this with the Navajos' cross-sign (89), in which the opposite movement (i.e., back towards the centre) is indicated.
A variation on this theme is the cross-form found in Auxerre (Eglise St-Germain). This has the same form drawn in a circle, but here with a reference to the chrism (90).
For most African tribes, the cross refers symbolically to the

---

*But it is only since the reign of Constantine that the cross can also refer to the historical fact of Christ's death on the Cross, and can acquire therefore an anthropomorphic meaning: 'Christ crucified'.

cosmos.

Again, the cross of St Andrew should also be read as an anthropomorphic sign that denotes man with outstretched arms and legs.

The cross-sign in mathematics is used for multiplication, and X, as a letter, stands for the unknown quantity. X can also mean: destroy, cancel, mark. In Roman numerals, X (= two times V, derived from the raised hand = 10) (91) is the sacred number of the Pythagoreans, meaning 'cosmos'. Compare this with the Chinese–Japanese ideogram in (80) and (92).

Both the Greek and Hebrew alphabets contain the X ('chi' and 'aleph' respectively). According to Houche, the cross-form X in the archaic Chinese means 'five': the four points of the compass plus the fifth point in the centre. This sign is found with a horizontal line above and below it, symbolizing the cosmic powers of yin and yang (92) in absolute harmony.

The superimposition of the Greek cross on the cross of St Andrew results in the cosmic solar-star sign, whose esoteric

86

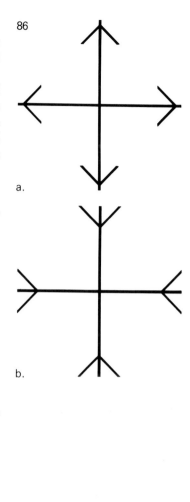

a.

b.

87

88

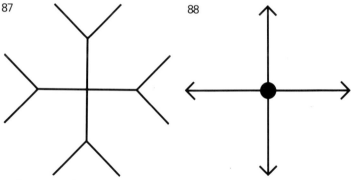

Stonemason's sign in the Palace of Diocletian. Split (Yugoslavia).

89   90   91

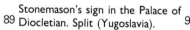

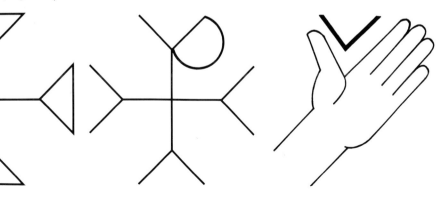

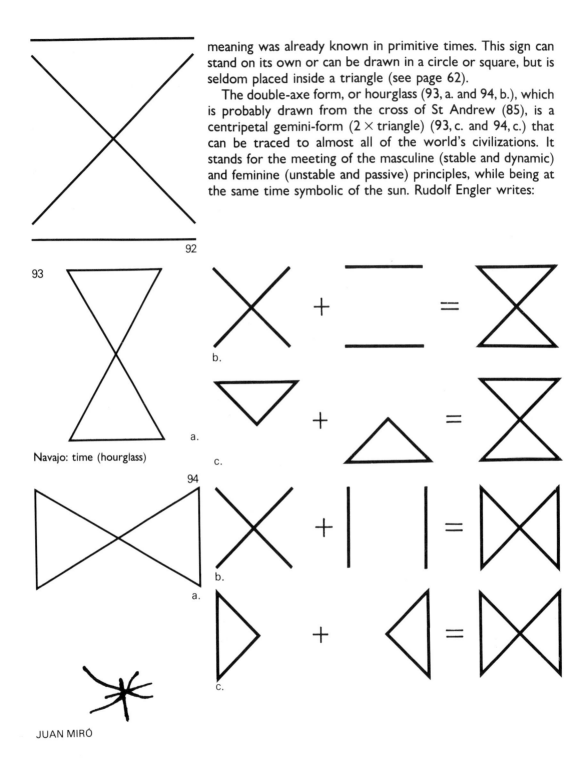

meaning was already known in primitive times. This sign can stand on its own or can be drawn in a circle or square, but is seldom placed inside a triangle (see page 62).

The double-axe form, or hourglass (93, a. and 94, b.), which is probably drawn from the cross of St Andrew (85), is a centripetal gemini-form (2 × triangle) (93, c. and 94, c.) that can be traced to almost all of the world's civilizations. It stands for the meeting of the masculine (stable and dynamic) and feminine (unstable and passive) principles, while being at the same time symbolic of the sun. Rudolf Engler writes:

92

93

Navajo: time (hourglass)

b.

c.

94

b.

a.

c.

a.

JUAN MIRÓ

74

Die Doppelaxt oder Doppelhammer sind Licht- und Sonnen-Symbole aus altnordisch-atlantischer Zeit. Dieser Kreuz-Zeichen aus der älteren Steinzeit ist der Vorgänger unseres Hammers. Es ist die altnordische Hiëroglyphe der Wintersonnenwende, in der das Licht der Welt wieder geboren wird resp. aufentsteht. Aus dieser Hiëroglyphe entsteht die heilige Doppelaxt, das von Norden her über die ganze Erde verbreitete höchste Symbol der Sonnengottheit. (?)

That the double axe, according to the Cabbala, is related to the *tan* (th) sign, which means 'cross', confirms its generally understood relationship to the cross itself, and therefore the morphological link with the sword-and-hammer (which likewise refers to the cross). The double-axe sign (*labrys*) appears frequently in Cretan culture (was it a royal sign for the domination of Minos over his people?), and some writers think it should be linked with the labyrinth.

In this symbol, also, a centripetal movement can be discerned, which is emphasized even more clearly in the double form, namely the Teutonic, Maltese or Coptic cross (95 and 96). This quaternary symbol is the sign too for the four Assyrian deities: Ra, Ano, Belos and Hera. In runic script, the double-axe sign (*dagos*) means 'day'.

The infinite, continuous figure 8, derived from the double-axe sign, is a lemniscate (the lemniscus is the Golden Ribbon) (97).

Until the middle of the 5th century B.C., the Greek letter *theta* was written as a cross in a circle (98, 1.), which, according to Herodotus, originated with the Phoenicians. Thereafter it became a circle, with at first a concentric point (the eye of God) (98, 2.), then, later, with a horizontal line (98, 3.).

A cross-in-a-circle is one of man's oldest universal symbols for the sun (the wheel of the sun), or for the spiritual division of the universe into four parts (98, 1.). The sign can also be read as a combination of the androgynous symbol of man within the infinity of the cosmos: the microcosmos within the macrocosmos. Graphically static yet magically powerful, this pagan sign went on to become one of the symbols and marks of recognition used by the first Christians. In Christian symbolism, the mid-point referred to Christ, the centre of everything, and the space around it to the four Evangelists.

Analogous symbolism is found in Eastern religions, where a higher value is also assigned to the centre, as the fifth element of something consisting of four parts. Rotated dynamically

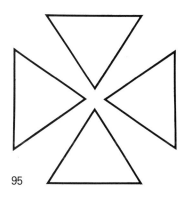

95

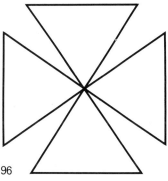

96

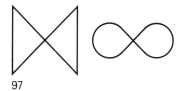

97

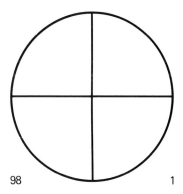

98   1

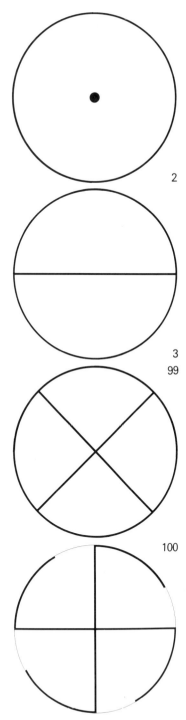

2

3
99

100

(99), it formed the basis for the chrism, which came into use during the reign of Constantine.*

In early Christian symbols found in the Roman catacombs, the swastika cross was derived from the cross-in-a-circle: by breaking the circumference of the circle, a kind of *crux dissimulata* (100) emerged. A further development was the *crux gammata* (102), as was the cross composed from the Greek letter *gamma* (the gammadion) (101). (See also page 101.) This cross, whose other name is *crux ansata* (handle-cross) was the symbol also for the central figure of Christ, the world's guiding force, surrounded by the four Evangelists.

A similar phenomenon is seen in the Tibetan sign, broken into its components: ⌐(phonetically, *sa*), ⌐ (also *sa*), ⌐ (*la*) and ⌐(*ra*).

All Christian cross-symbolism was adopted initially from pagan sun-symbolism, and only later under Constantine did it acquire its reference to the historical fact of Christ's crucifixion. STAT CRUX DUM VOLVITUR ORBIS: the Cross of Christ reincarnated marks the end of pagan cosmology's timeless tradition, whereby the cross represents the sun, moon, stars and cosmos. Christianity eliminates the threatening, rotating aspect of the cross by immobilizing it in a more stable vertical–horizontal symbol. The cross, with its undertones of law and constancy, will save mankind from the vicissitudes of paganism.

Originally, 98, 1., 99 and 100, as well as 101 and 102, represented respectively also the wheel, the sun-wheel, the rota, the sun and the light—the wheel of fate and li.e. They retained this significance throughout prehistory, on Crete, among the Hittites and all over the Far East. The more obvious wheel-like sun symbol (103) is, of course, a combination of 98, 1. and 99: a union of passive and active, with the same meanings as 98, 99 and 100 (see pages 81, 82 and 83).

Some writers hold that forms of the cross frequently induced the development of the circle (quadrangle/octagon/rotation) (106). (See also page 101.)

It would, in any event, seem reasonable to link the sun-

*The first stage was the chrism (I for *Jesous* and X for *Christos*). Later the top of the I acquired a small curve, or loop, so becoming *rho*. Added to the X-cross, the X (chi) + P (rho) became an abbreviation of *Christos*. A similar connection is seen with the Egyptian life-sign (the Horus-loop), where a christianized variant originated in the rho + the horizontal-line ⚓.

wheel (the notion of the solstice) with evolution leading up to and, indeed, beyond the swastika (tetraskelion), together with sun symbols, and symbols of cosmic order and harmony in man himself. Frequently the angular swastika is derived from the rounded one (107 and 108), but a reverse development is just as likely, although, in practice, rare. It may

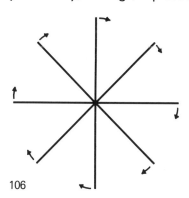

106

also be that the two forms developed independently but in parallel, from different roots.

In Sanskrit, the sauvastika, sauwastika or swavastika rotates to the left (109, a.b.), and the swastika to the right (110, a.b.). This truly archetypal form, though having undoubtedly different origins, is found in Greece, Egypt, Africa, Crete, Mycenae, India and China ... right through to Ireland, the Celtic world, Lithuania,* Tibet, Pre-Columbian America, the Eskimos, the Christian cultures ... through all the ages of man, in fact, from

*In Lithuanian, which, among European languages, is closest to the Sanskrit, the word *swastika* means 'well-being'.

107   108

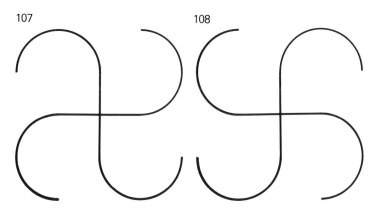

101

102

Tibet
Alaska
Seminole indians (North Carolina, USA)
Müncheberg (3rd-century A.D.)

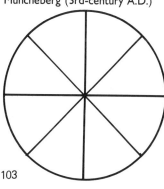

103

104: see top image, page 83.
105: see top image, page 81, and middle image, page 82

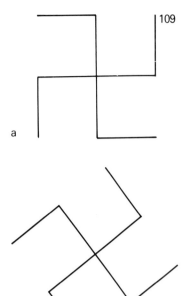

a

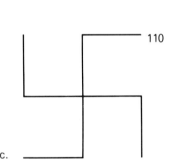

b. SAUVASTIKA

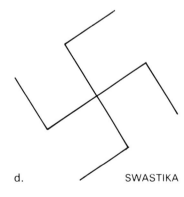

c.

d. SWASTIKA

109

110

prehistory to the 20th century.

In Chinese, the swastika was called *lei-wen*, which means 'thunderbolt', and is therefore also a reference to a heavenly phenomenon. They adopted the sign from the Indians and gave it the meaning: 'The ten-thousand gods'.

Sometimes this gamma-cross is a symbol of fertility and prosperity—a lucky sign, therefore. But it can also be simply a talisman, or even a prophylactic. Some writers see in it a union of male and female (J. Hoffman), others a symbol for the phallus, and yet others a symbol for the female principle, a sign of fertility. According to Sir George Birdwood in *Report on the Old Records of the India Office* (London, 1981), for the Hindus the swastika is the symbol for *Ganesh* (the male principle): sun, light, life; the sauvastika is *Kali* (the female principle): darkness, death, destruction. The first-mentioned is related to the path of the sun from east to west, the second from west to east.

It is possible that the swastika reached China and Japan and became widespread via Buddhism, although it had probably already existed previously in the primitive cultures of those countries.

The swastika is a dynamic image, especially in its rotating form (109, b., 110, b.), often appearing with little (walking) feet attached to its ends (111) to strengthen its mechanical dynamism, and rotating also around the axis at its point of intersection. It is hardly a coincidence that this sign is called *fylfot* (multiple feet) in Anglo-Saxon.

The swastika is very popular in Romanian folk-art. Some call the sign *vîrtelnita*, referring to its turning and rotating (*a se invîrti* = to turn, to rotate).

The swastika, with hundreds of variants and infinite combinations, must rank among man's most fertile signs, whether used in religious and magical symbolism, in cosmic imagery or in ornamental art. In these accompanying illustrations, I have tried, by placing a few special types of swastika next to one another, to demonstrate the graphic origins of the swastika.

Fascism saw in the swastika rune a dynamic, obsessive force, a symbol of optimism to mark the glorious march forward of the Aryan race in its struggle against the spiritually higher, cabbalistic, Jewish sign, the *Magon David*.

The triskele, triskelion or *triquetra* (three-legged swastika)

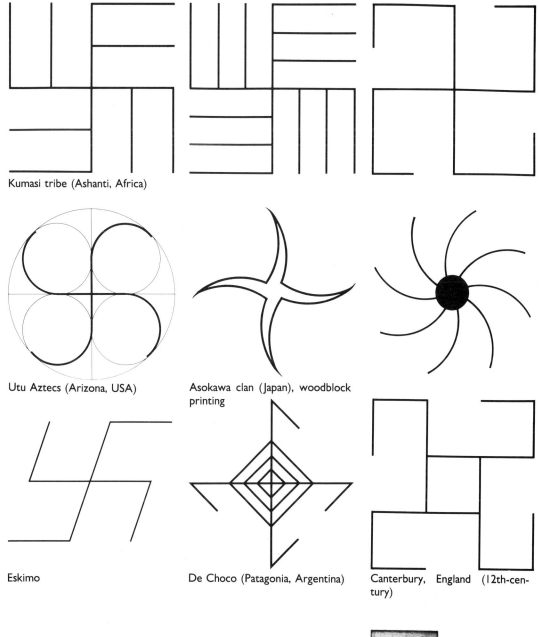

Kumasi tribe (Ashanti, Africa)

Utu Aztecs (Arizona, USA)

Asokawa clan (Japan), woodblock printing

Eskimo

De Choco (Patagonia, Argentina)

Canterbury, England (12th-century)

Ashanti gold-weight

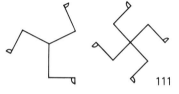

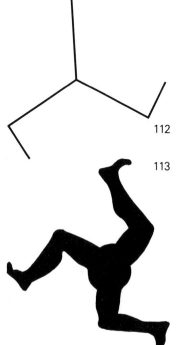

111

112

113

(112) is related to the swastika, although less widely found; it can also be connected with the sun or moon.

In Greece, the triskelion meant progress and victory, and was found with naturalistically drawn legs (113) on the shield of Enceladus. In Celtic culture the triskele mostly had a spiral structure (New Grange, County Meath, Ireland). This triskele is also found in Cretan linear script, where it is developed from a squarer, hieroglyphic style of drawing.

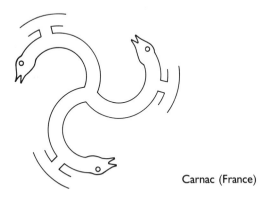

Carnac (France)

Left: Hiberno–Saxon figure (9th-century), found in the Oseberg burial ship (Norway); originally it was the handle of a bowl. Swastikas can be seen in the four corners of the cross. (Bygdoy Museum, Oslo, Norway).

Below: Decorative pattern in a Roman villa in Sussex, England.

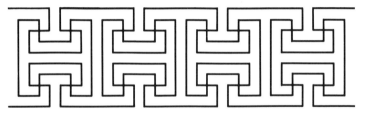

Elementary combinations of the
cross and three basic forms:

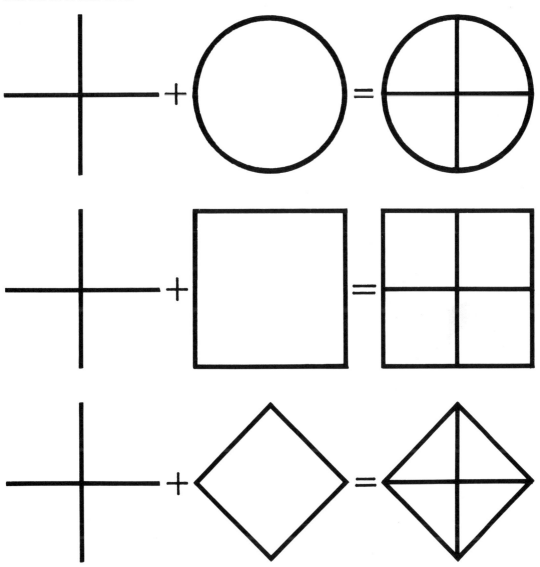

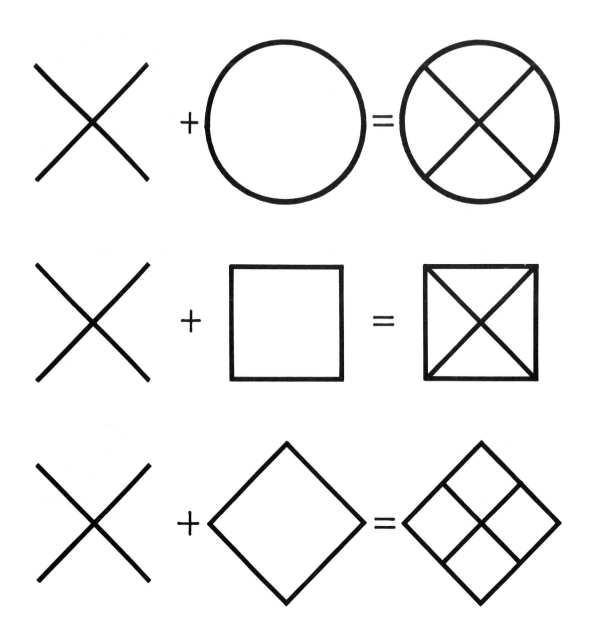

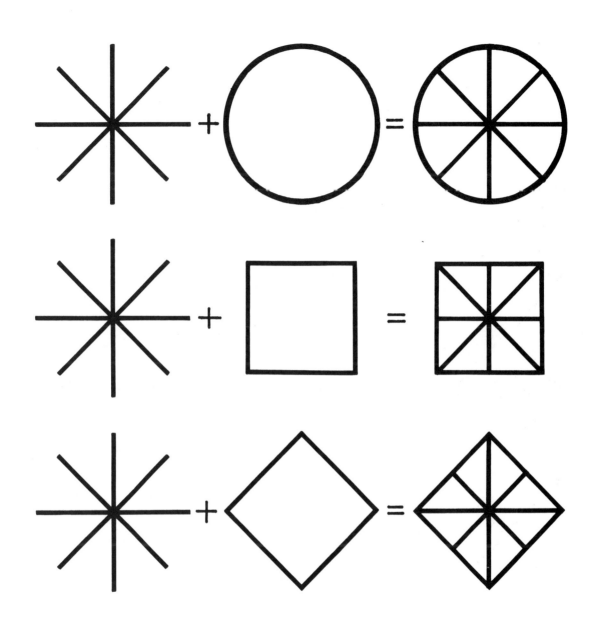

Spray-paint graffito in New York's
Central Park. As primitive as any
spiral petroglyph, this form is obviously produced with motor stimu-
lation as the generative force, and
is drawn for *le plaisir de l'acte* from
the centre outwards.

CHAPTER 3

THE BASIC FORMS:
CIRCLE—SQUARE—TRIANGLE

Τὸ γὰρ εὖ παρὰ μικρὸν διὰ πολλῶν ἀριθμῶν γίγνεσθαι.

Polykleitos (5th century B.C.)

Geometry is God Himself.
J. Kepler (1571–1630)

Fig 46
Gibon Sengai
The Universe, Kakemono
Idemitsu Collection, Tokyo, Japan

86

CIRCLE—SQUARE—TRIANGLE

When those basic forms, the circle, square and triangle, first appear in any civilization, a critical period of change ensues. In its own way, discovering these basic forms is of the same level of importance for the development of a civilization as the invention of the wheel, which changed completely the technical and industrial evolution of man.

Fundamentally, the arrival of the circle, square and triangle signals the attainment of a higher level of intelligence and culture, while at the same time the door opens for masses of new communicative and creative possibilities. Gradually, through intense, spontaneous use, these shapes attain the status of formal visual symbols. They become an intellectual game, and with that development a whole civilization can make an important step forward.

Such a development marks a stage in the growth of man's humanity. Another way to put it is that from the moment these basic forms are discovered, human culture, acquires a clearly discernible historic evolution as a result of the newly developed intellectual processes they entail: *Homo sapiens* takes a firm grip on his developmental potential, and categorically emerges from his primitive state. But in Western civilization it took until Euclid (*The Elements of Geometry*, Alexandria, 300 B.C.), the disciple of Pythagoras, before we can really talk of 'geometry' (which means, in Greek, 'surveying'). The practical application of geometry, however, dates from Vitruvius (5th century B.C.).

From these mechanistic games, *Homo ludens*, using native manual dexterity, cultivates symbol and form, and in so doing masters the basic forms. Preoccupied at first with his own craftsmanship, he suddenly recognizes the power inherent in what he is drawing. With a mixture of intuition and dawning awareness, primitive man initially manipulates the basic forms, so expressing his primeval angst over his inability to comprehend the unknown, or to communicate with the superhuman: the cosmos, the principle of life, the divinity.

At this animistic stage, use of these shapes is monopolized by a caste of priests or chieftains, or by exclusive sects, or secret societies, with the intention of manipulating and exorcizing these higher powers. Only later, after familiarity has inevitably set in, do these forms become adopted by private individuals as a medium of ordinary communication, becoming simple signs, stripped of magic and mystery, that refer to workaday reality.

The next stage in this process of familiarization is the use of the basic forms as elements of decoration, devoid of any significance. Now they have become no more than an abstract game for the artist, to be applied in ceramics, textiles, weaving, home or furniture decoration. It is evident in this last phase that the artist-craftsman has more than simply aesthetic intentions: he seeks, rather, to give the object his personal hallmark, and attempts to lift the object above the level of impersonal uniformity.

With the passage of time, the basic forms and signs may lose their original meaning, or else this meaning may be forgotten. Later they may suddenly acquire either their original meaning again, or else a totally new one, and are therefore resurrected from their mundane role of abstract decoration, to be manipulated anew on the level of magic, religion or communication.

This evolving process of familiarization is most clear with the basic forms, for they are universal, recognized spontaneously as magic signs, and often follow a parallel development in similar but separate cultures. Other primal signs can also follow the same process (the cross, double axe, etc.).

The rational qualities and functional potential of the triangle and square contrast strongly with the spiritual value of the circle, whose roots lie in feeling and emotion. So while the circle may have a strong spiritual and symbolic function, this tends to be far less often the case with the other two forms.

Often the primitive artist uses the basic forms, especially the circle and square, as a kind of enclosure, a fence (*enclos*) to protect what is enclosed against intruders and non-initiates.

From the moment when the basic forms are first deliberately applied in an area where they have special significance beyond simply what we call 'the graphic techniques', whether this is in geometry, algebra, any of the sciences, architecture, alchemy or astrology, or when they serve as a point of departure for such rational concepts as measurement, proportion, comparability or relationship, a civilization reaches a higher plane of knowledge. Historically this is the moment when identifiable intellectual personalities appear, people such as Pythagoras (Samos, 580 B.C.) and Ptolemy (Alexandria, 150 B.C.).

The Arabic philosophers regarded the development of the triangle (3: threefold) as a product of human intelligence derived from the straight line (2: twofold), which itself developed out of the splitting of the point (1: oneness). The triangle symbolizes the link between heaven and earth. If the apex of the triangle points downwards, it means the active link, directed towards heaven; if the apex points upwards, it is an active link directed at the earth. The superimposition of these two triangles, Solomon's seal, the dynamic hexagon, is the union of both opposing forces.

In traditional Arabic philosophic systems, such as Sufism, the triangle occupies prime place among the forms. In Buddhism too the triangle is the first (human) form, preceded only by the circle, but here it is spiritually cosmic, belonging to another order. According to Tantric teaching, the order of the forms is: the square (earth: heavy, rough, hard, slow, compact ...); the circle (water: liquid, permeable, cold, soft ...); the triangle (fire: hot, light, dry, clear ...); the sickle of the moon (air: light, cold, dry, transparent ...); and the point (ether: light, weightless, elastic ...).

In the traditional Western view the succession is: circle, square, triangle. But Klee proposes instead: square, triangle, circle. According to Pythagoras, the number 4 is the first fixed structural, fundamental concept. Euclid, however, links the number 4 to the static square. Dynamically, 4 will become the cross.

In the postscript of the previously quoted *Ryakuga Haya Oshie*, Hokusai maintains that all signs originate from the circle and the square, and that all compositions should thus be tackled with a rule and compass. Hokusai probably arrived at this conclusion following contact with Western (Dutch) examples, or perhaps by way of Chu Ryo's *Kômô Zatsua* (Edo, 1787), which shows Western influence.

At the opening of this chapter (page 86) is that masterly calligraphic drawing, *The Universe*, by Gibon Sengai, the great Zen abbot of the Shofukuji temple at Hakata (Kyushu) (1750–

Rosicrucian symbolic drawing (17th-century engraving).
The outer circle represents the macrocosm, without beginning and without end. The triangle symbolizes the dual or binary nature of man and the world, which converges at the topmost point: perfection. The circle with two human figures represents the microcosm, dominated by the macrocosm. The square surrounding it represents stability, security, safety.

!837). For this Zen master and genius, the circle-triangle-square were a condensed expression of the 1-2-3 evolution, which no language can codify so succinctly and intelligently: the circle (the endless self, without beginning, without end); the triangle (the first form, origin of all forms); the square, times two, or times four. The triangle (the 'ten-thousand things', as the Chinese philosophers called it), is also infinitely evolving and changing. It is a graphic masterpiece, as well as an obsessional subject for meditation. The monumental importance of this painting derives from the fact that only a sage like Sengai, who truly understands that humour is the essential antithesis of the sacred (or the transcendental, according to Herbert Read), could produce such a masterpiece.

Sengai draws the circle and triangle clearly and with determination, whereas the square is watery, blurred, affected already by the other two forms: it is not even a square with equal sides! It is the start of an immense cosmic game: a prelude to the infinite.

PAUL KLEE
AND THE BASIC FORMS

Between 1922 and 1925 in the Bauhaus, that great art-laboratory, Paul Klee evolved his celebrated theory of basic forms. Possessed of rare intuition and great depth of educational experience, he succeeded over this period in developing—and elaborated subsequently—a properly functional system.

Klee's writings belong with the theories of Kandinsky and Delaunay at the very foundation of 20th-century art, in being a first attempt at making a scientific approach to the elements of art. I reproduce here Klee's theory by way of homage to this pioneering theorist of forms.

According to Klee's system, forms can be arranged in vertical columns: in column 1 ('actual') are the square, triangle and circle; in the corresponding positions in column 2 ('casual') are the cross, inverted T and star-shape; and following them, reading across, are the combined elements of columns 1 and 2.

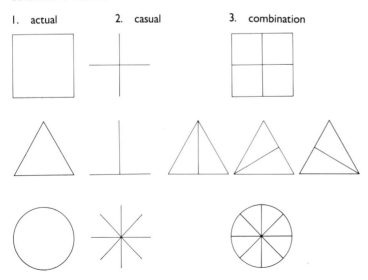

1. actual   2. casual   3. combination

THE CIRCLE

If it is true that for most civilizations the circle, square and triangle are marked out as religious, philosophical, magical, astrological and cosmic symbols, then this is especially the case for the circle. So generous in form is the circle (115) that it can be easily made to symbolize a mass of subjects, within any given pattern of civilization, on a variety of different levels, their interpretation depending on the context in which the circle is being manipulated. For this reason, the circle is mostly found as glyph, pictogram, ideogram, astrogram or phonogram.

The many qualities of the circle—the constant relationship between centre and the never-ending, continuous circumference—make it a highly fascinating, obsessive form, one which can refer at one and the same time to the cyclical passage of time*, the movement of heavenly bodies and of the cosmos, the limit of the void, emptiness or completeness...

Pythagoras and Plato spoke of the circle as the most beautiful of all the forms. Simply by dipping into the symbolism that is linked to the circle, we can form an idea of its timeless, universal utility:

THE CIRCLE: GOD—SUN—COSMOS—UNIVERSE—EARTH—
HEAVEN—ALL—NOTHING (CABBALA: AYIN = NON-THING)—
ENDLESS—YONI (SHRI-YANTRA)—HIGHEST POWER (TAO)—
PRINCIPLE OF LIFE—VULVA—ANUS—UNITY—FERTILITY—
SIMPLICITY—EMPTINESS—FULLNESS—PERFECTION—HOLE—
WOMAN—MOTHER—BREAST(S)—STOMACH—NAVEL—
SOURCE—END—WHEEL—TIME—I—MOVEMENT—
SUPERHUMAN—LIGHT—DAY—WARMTH—COMPASS—
FORMLESSNESS—NIMBUS—ZODIAC—GOLD—HEAD—EYE—

---

*Some systems consider time as a circular, cyclical process; others as a linear and discursive one; others still as a moment that is forever returning to itself.

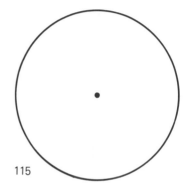

115

Crete
Sanskrit
Slieve-na-Calliagh, Ireland

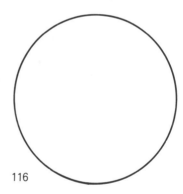

116

Fig 50 (opposite)
On the tombstones of the Bogomil sect in Bosnia–Hercegovina (Radimlja) can be found single scratch ornamentation and zig-zag lines. Especially remarkable is the head with concentric circles, on the smaller stone, and the V-shapes on the arms of the warrior on the larger stone.

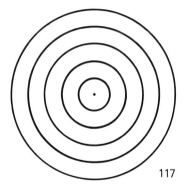

117

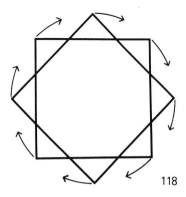

118

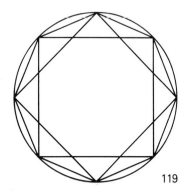

119

On the one hand, we can imagine the circle as an extension of that smallest unit of form, the point: the image of a stone thrown into water (117). On the other, the circle can be created by rotating around a single central point the four corners of a square or the four points of a cross (118). I have already noted when discussing the spiral that the circle originated from a primal, mechanical hand-movement, and therefore possibly can be seen as evolving from the spiral, in the sequence: hand-movement—spiral—concentric rings—circle.

Many writers regard the octagon (= future life) as an intermediate stage between the square and circle (119). Could the progression possibly be: centre-point, N–E–S–W (square or diamond)—NE–SE–SW–NW (octagon)—circle? Is not the circle, in the mind's eye, a square without corners? Or is the square perhaps a circle with square corners? But whereas the square has a N–E–S–W orientation, the circle actually lacks any direction whatever.

This leads on to the mathematical game of squaring the circle, the alchemists' quest, which obsessed mankind for centuries: the square, the circle, the union of opposites...

In mysticism, the snake that bites its own tail (*ouroboros*, Greek: tail-biter) is the symbol for 0—cause and effect; according to the Book of Genesis, the sacred wisdom itself (120): 'at my end is my beginning'—simultaneously alpha and omega. The Gnostics, especially the Naässian sect (*naäs* = snake), link this sign (*ouroboros*) with the cyclic wheel. One half of the snake is white, the other half black (comparable to yin-yang): an amalgam of active/passive; constructive/destructive; positive/negative; good/evil; god/devil.

In the Cabbala, the Kronos-snake (*nachash*) bites its own tail, just as the Satan snake does, which must devour and so destroy itself. This is the Messianic principle: evil destroys itself and in so doing liberates mankind from evil.

According to the Cabbala, *ouroboros* also meant Satan and wisdom simultaneously. Lao Tse states that in India the *ouroboros* was the origin of the triumvirate: Brahma (creation), Vishnu (preservation) and Shiva (destruction). In Western culture the *ouroboros* likewise is a death-symbol found on gravestones from antiquity right up to the present day: a symbol for salvation, welfare, rebirth, the redemption of evil... The wreaths laid in cemeteries may have their origins in this primeval sign. Indeed, the phenomenon of the *ouroboros* is universal, it is found in the cultures of the Mayans, North American Indians, Dogons of Mali, Ancient Greeks and Celts; it occurs throughout the East, and in Western alchemy...

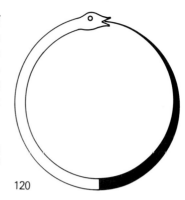

120

In Gothic cathedrals the circle was invaluable. Used as a zodiac or rosette, it was the perfect vehicle for depicting a cycle of events, enabling a narrative to develop in hierarchical stages, reading either from the centre out to the circumference or in reverse.

In ancient Korean script, the circle meant: 'throat'. In the alphabetical *han'gul* script (where it is phonetically *a*) it is equivalent to ○.

For the great Zen abbot Sengai, the circle represented infinity, the origin of all beings—but infinity itself is formless. In Zen art there are still circle calligraphies (the Japanese Ensó) used by great artists such as Jiun, Gocho, Tórei and Bankei: symbols of enlightenment and wisdom.

In Egyptian hieroglyphic script, the circle with a point at the centre was a sign of the sun, the deity Ra, which can be linked to agriculture (fertility) in the Nile region, and the annual depositing of silt during that river's flood.

In Mayan pictographic and astrographic script, the circle without a centre means 'the sun'. Used as an ideogram, it stands for light, for warmth and day; phonetically it is *kin* (phonogram) and *ah* (alphabet).

In ancient Chinese, however, the circle with a centre stands for 'sun' (see page 64). And in the West also, the medieval alchemists and astrologers used the circle with a centre as a symbol for sun and for gold (*aurum*).

The circle means yoni (vulva) in the Shri-yantra (Tantrism), and the dot (*bindu*) in its centre is the seed or sperm (energy). The yoni gives birth to the world and to time, while the lingam (male organ) is the producer of the seed of *being*.

With the Dogons of Mali, the circle (pot with fire = matrix) stands for the sun, with a (copper) spiral (= sperm) wound eight times around it, this being a fertility symbol.

Indonesian mythology (Lauré Danö) also has the image of the snake, which encloses a barrel (the world) like a ring (J. P. Barbier).

95

The meeting (intersections) of two circles produces the mandorla, resulting in the almond shape (*vesica piscis*) (121), the fish—vulva-symbol, referring in many civilizations to the vulva and fertility. But it frequently happens that the mandorla is at one and the same time a symbol for the vulva, the eye and the mouth—organs which in an erotic-symbolic context are often interchanged because of their morphological similarities.

If a vertical line crosses the middle (123, 1.), symbolizing the closed vulva, the sign also acquires the meaning of 'denial', and therefore also of 'infertility'; whereas the mandorla that contains a point ('opening', or also 'seed', 'sperm') will mean 'fertility' (123, 2.). The horizontal mandorla with a point means 'eye' (of God), 'the open eye' (123, 3.). With a transverse horizontal line crossing the middle, it means 'the closed eye' (123, 4.). Small wonder then that so often there should be such confusion regarding symbolism of the eye and vulva...

In Christian iconography, the mandorla is often used to enshrine (enclos/nimbus) the Holy Virgin, Christ or the saints (fig. 48). For the early Christians, the *ichthys* (fish) (*Iesous Christos Theou Yios Soter*) was the symbol for Christ (122).

There is an obvious relationship between the morphology of the mandorla, circle and oval on the one hand, and that of the rhomboid on the other. There is an evident symbolic relationship too, for example in Western heraldry, in which the oval means 'écu des dames', and the diamond 'écu des demoiselles'.

In Tantrism, all spheroids, and therefore all ovals too, are cosmic symbols.

Fig 47
Grande Dame, a Russian folk sculpture from the Kargapol district (c.1930), made of clay. Note the mandorla–vulva symbol on her dress.

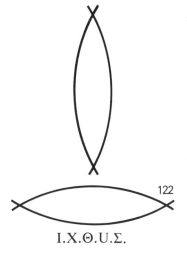

I.X.Θ.U.Σ.

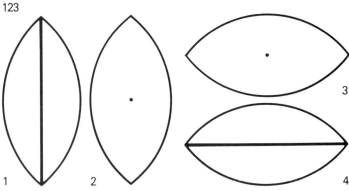

123

1

2

3

4

122

The circle is a flat surface, limited by a single line, in such a way that all lines that start from one point inside the form and fall inside it and onto the line will be equal among themselves. That point is called the centre of the circle. Euclid—*Elements*

The circle possesses strong mnemonic properties, and is therefore a remarkably functional sign. It is used today in signals, traffic-management techniques, graphic symbols, publicity artwork, and so on. Think, too, of those present-day artists in whose work the circle is a basic element: Dekkers, Mangold, van Severen, Vasarely, Seuphor, Delaunay, Peter Sedgley, Dogottex, Nicholson, Noland...

Maybe it is because of its cosmic, metaphysical and mystic background that the circle has such extensive graphical value, and is so durable. This would explain its origins in the remote past and its continued strong presence today.

Of course, the strongly sensual and aesthetic qualities of the circle have some part to play in this, and can hardly be neglected: its flawlessness, perfection, purity of form, dynamic tension, mechanical qualities, subtlety, communicative power, naturalness... No form is as sensitive as the circle. Any slight alteration causes it to lose its original qualities.

Unlike the square, it has no direction, but the instant one places a cross within its circumference, it becomes a compass (124). The circle rotates dynamically, but let one single point appear on the circumference, or any interruption appear, and this dynamism is arrested (125) (126).

Visually, the circle is highly active, and aggressively demands attention. It requires flawless execution and technical skill on the part of its maker. There is a charming story about the emissary of Pope Benedictus IX, who asked Giotto for some

Fig 48
Detail of a miniature from the *Liber Floridus* of Wolfenbüttel. The lamb is surrounded by a double nimbus-protection (*enclos*), the mandorla and the circle, each one doubled and intertwined.

Fig 49
Nimbus. Indian miniature (19th-century).

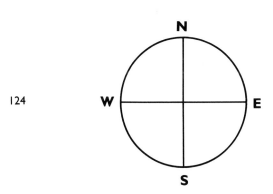

124

proof of his skill. Giotto drew a circle (the O of Giotto) in one single movement as a proof for His Holiness, and was rewarded with a commission to paint the five famous episodes from the life of Christ.

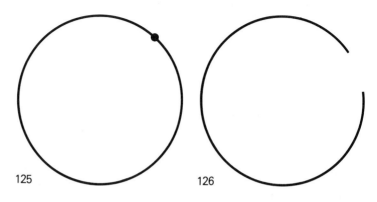

125   126

Children's graffiti on a wall near a school. The circles were drawn spontaneously, with a natural 45° rotation at a height of about 1.2 metres.

THE SQUARE

Rectilinear figures are those that are enclosed within straight lines. Four-sided forms are those that are contained by four straight lines. Among the four-sided forms, the equilateral rectangle is the square.
Euclid—*Elements*

There is much in common between those two basic forms, the square (127) and the circle ('circle = square'). But there are also many contradictions: circle = spirituality, square = chthonic (relating to the underworld); circle = cyclical time, square = static. The two in combination (128, 1–3.) mean the material principle (square) within the totality (circle), the conjunction of the earthly and the spiritual (*conjunctio*). The relationship between the two forms, with its underlying confusions, can often be indicated so starkly (as, for example, in their anarchic use as equivalent signs in the Numidian and Saharan scripts) that their relationship is in fact quite clear, despite their morphologically opposite natures and qualities.

But when the rotated, unstable, dynamic square—the diamond—is superimposed upon the stable, static, straight square, symbolic associations arise, comparable to the symbolism of the Cabbalistic Seal of Solomon. They imply the unity of opposite concepts, yet ones that are often complementary: for example, stability and instability, spirit and matter, man and woman, heaven and earth. Such oppositions are anihilated when you reach the centre: the point where stability and tranquillity lie: equilibrium (128, 4.).

Whereas the circle originated spontaneously out of mechanical movements of the human hand, the square, rather, is a quaternary product arising from a rational process of construction, namely, connecting up of four points, or placing four lines squarely (orthogonally) on top of one another; these are either two vertical and two horizontal lines (129, a.b.), or four corners joined up (90°) (129, c.d.e.). The centre-point originates from crossed diagonals (the fifth point; cf. *quincunx*).

Here, then, lies the correlation with the circle—for a circle, with the same centre, can also be constructed through the same four (corner) points. Here, too, are strong references to the four points of the compass, and to the *I* (the

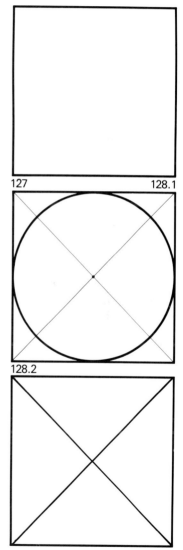

127   128.1

128.2

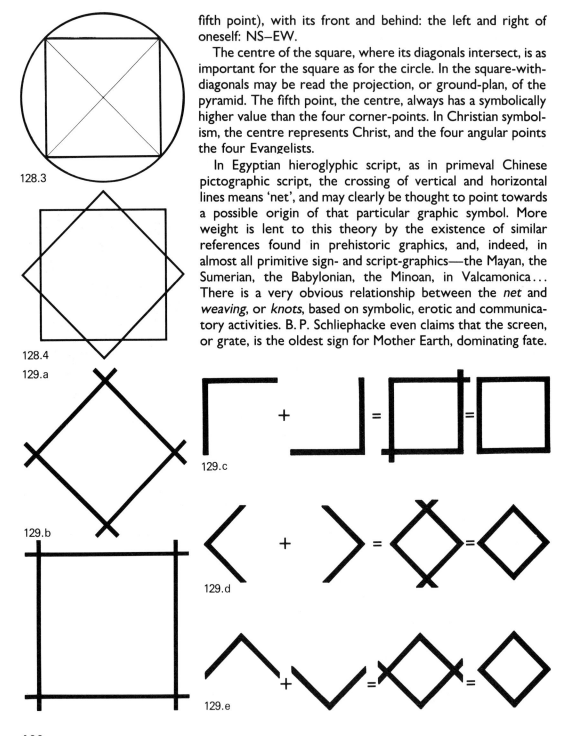

128.3

128.4

129.a

129.b

129.c

129.d

129.e

fifth point), with its front and behind: the left and right of oneself: NS–EW.

The centre of the square, where its diagonals intersect, is as important for the square as for the circle. In the square-with-diagonals may be read the projection, or ground-plan, of the pyramid. The fifth point, the centre, always has a symbolically higher value than the four corner-points. In Christian symbolism, the centre represents Christ, and the four angular points the four Evangelists.

In Egyptian hieroglyphic script, as in primeval Chinese pictographic script, the crossing of vertical and horizontal lines means 'net', and may clearly be thought to point towards a possible origin of that particular graphic symbol. More weight is lent to this theory by the existence of similar references found in prehistoric graphics, and, indeed, in almost all primitive sign- and script-graphics—the Mayan, the Sumerian, the Babylonian, the Minoan, in Valcamonica… There is a very obvious relationship between the *net* and *weaving*, or *knots*, based on symbolic, erotic and communicatory activities. B. P. Schliephacke even claims that the screen, or grate, is the oldest sign for Mother Earth, dominating fate.

Elsewhere again, in Egyptian hieroglyphic script, the screen was a symbol for field, or for house; as it is also in modern Chinese, where the sign—derived from the archaic sign (130)—clearly refers to a cosmic (Taoistic) field.

But it is very possible that the square/diamond originates by simply connecting up the extremes of the NE–SW compass bearings (132, a.)—although the intention might also be to localize the N, E, S and W sides, so letting the corners fall at the NE–SE–SW–NW (132, b.). The rotating square/diamond shape (133) alludes to the circle (and, *a fortiori*, to the octagon). Is it any wonder that these two forms became such an obsession for the alchemists? Besides pursuing the *aurum philosophicum*, they also sought after the *quadratura circuli*: a Western mandala, an attempt at uniting matter and spirit in such a way as to bring equilibrium into the cosmos and, at the same time, into the *spiritus* (fig. 40). The *quadratura circuli* can also be interpreted as, literally, the end of the world: the dynamic, cosmic (spiritual) circle is about to die, ending in the static (material) earthly square.

In the gammadion sign (a square formed by the Greek letter *gamma*; in Arabic, the 5 *arkân* = the 5 corners), the cross is vertical–horizontal. In Christian symbolism, this would, once again, signify Christ standing between the four

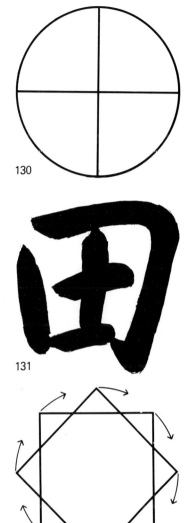

130

131

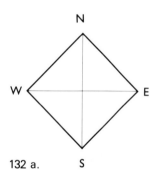

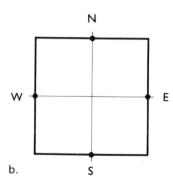

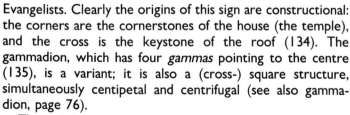

132 a.

b.

133

Evangelists. Clearly the origins of this sign are constructional: the corners are the cornerstones of the house (the temple), and the cross is the keystone of the roof (134). The gammadion, which has four *gammas* pointing to the centre (135), is a variant; it is also a (cross-) square structure, simultaneously centipetal and centrifugal (see also gamma-dion, page 76).

The anti-dynamic square can have nearly as many symbolic meanings as the circle:

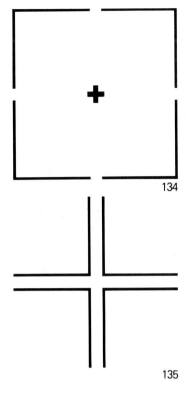

THE SQUARE: GOD—BODY—EARTH—COSMOS (CHRISTIANITY)—
WORLD—NATURE (ASTROLOGY)—MATTER—REALITY—MAN
(BIOLOGY)—THORAX (BIOLOGY)—MASCULINE—NIMBUS—
MATTER—HORIZON—LODGE (FREEMASONRY)—NEW MOON
(ASTRONOMY)—SALT (PARACELSUS)—LIGHT (ALCHEMY)—
QUADRATURE—THE FOUR ELEMENTS (FIRE–AIR–WATER–EARTH)—
SENSORY PERCEPTION—INTUITION—FEELING—THINKING
(JUNG)—SOLIDITY—STABILITY—PROTECTION—
ORGANIZATION—CONSTRUCTION—RATIO—HARMONY
(PLATO)—ENCLOSURE (ENCLOS)—EYE OF GOD (OJO DE DIOS)—
FRAME—WINDOW—COIN (CHINESE: JEN)—GATEWAY—SOUL
(PYTHAGORAS)—TRUTH (JAPANESE: SHIN)...

134

135

136

However masculine the square might be as a symbol in
Western civilization, the Eastern civilizations, such as the
Chinese and the Hindu, see the square as a feminine symbol,
relating to the earth and fertility. With a point in the middle
(136), or with a horizontal line through it, as in modern
Chinese script, it also sometimes becomes, just like the circle,
a sun-symbol (63). In Chinese Li Ssu and Kou Ssu, the square
means 'mouth' (137).

In the Korean *han'gul* script, the square □ (phonetically, m)
was derived from an even older □ sign, which represented
the contour of the mouth.

Strangely, in the West, the diamond shape (138), or
rotated square, has acquired a more feminine, dynamic sense,
which again links closely with the circle and mandorla (Freud:
vulva). Similar references to feminity can be found also among
the Baule of the Ivory Coast, West Africa. For the African
Bambaras, a rounded diamond, with a point inside it, means
the sex of a young girl (139). And women in Guatemala
weave diamonds into their skirts, referring pointedly to their
sex.

Frequently, however, the diamond, with or without a point
in the middle, can also mean 'eye' (the eye of God). The
diamond also figures in the symbolism of the runic signs:
Ingwos, the god Ingw, ancestor of the Unäonen (pho-
neticized).

Jung recognizes in the square a surplus value of the triangle
(3 + 1), while in Christianity, the square symbolizes the four
Evangelists, with Christ at the centre (cf. *quincunx*) (140). In
hagiography, the still-living saints wear a square nimbus. But
the square as a religious symbol is much less common than the
circle—not only in Christianity, but also in most religions.

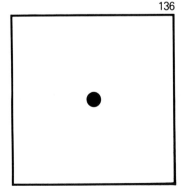

Sengai says that the square is the first product of the triangle (one triangle, times two) (141). This reduplication can continue infinitely, and is called by the Chinese philosophers 'the ten-thousand things', by which they mean: the universe, the cosmos. Taking this theme a stage further, we can also say that the square is the product of four isosceles triangles.

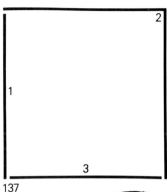

137

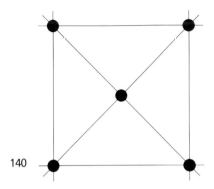

140

Westerners, by contrast, are more inclined to assert that the triangle comes out of a halved square, or one quartered by diagonals (142). Naturally, these are right-angled triangles.

The square, as a practical device, has many uses. It can isolate something (for example, a text, or an image), or focus attention upon it. It is a frame, a window. Manipulated graphically, it can visually protect whatever it encloses, against the (visual) influence of whatever surrounds it. In both magic and religion, the square bars the way to the profane, protecting the enclosed against aggression and indiscretion, at the same time enhancing the magical or sacred force of the surface within.

138

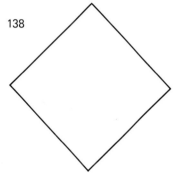

139

141

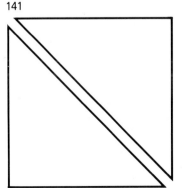

142

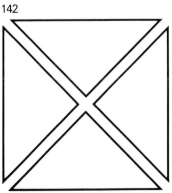

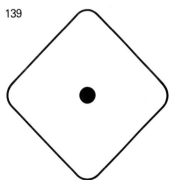

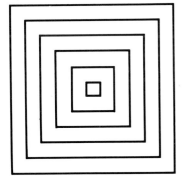

143

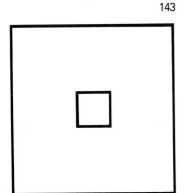

144

The circle also has all these qualities, but by its very nature the square is different, being hard-edged, more radical, more aggressive, more solid . . . a symbol of intelligence. The square, a rational and functional form, is architectonically of enormous value. It is used especially in cube form by sedentary populations, whereas nomadic populations resort rather to the cone, which is a circular and triangular form, the combination of circle and triangle.

Concentric squares are found in yantras and mandalas; in the prehistoric drawings of Capo di Ponte, in Italy; and often in the ground plans of various architectural structures, such as temples, and urban plans (143). In South America, the sign of a diamond (concentric diamond) acquires the meaning of *Ojo de Dios* (the eye of God). In the Chinese–Japanese sign-script (144), the similar sign means: once, one time; or: surround, enclose (see page 64).

In 20th-century art, we think of *Black Square on White* (1915) and *White Square on White* (1918) by Malevich; of the square structures of Mondrian and van Doesburg; of the obsessive squares of Albers, Max Bill, Richard P. Lohse, Vasarely, Franz Kline, Tapies, Stella, Ad Reinhardt . . .

THE TRIANGLE

Rectilinear figures are those enclosed within straight lines. Trilateral forms are those that lie within the borders formed by three straight lines. Euclid—*Elements*

The three-point motif (145) is a universal, ever-present, visually arresting sign. Physically perceived, it is then easily completed in the imagination (*gestalt*): the three points are connected by imaginary lines so that they actually read as a triangle (146). It is natural to start with three points before moving on to the triangle—for often they have analogous meanings.

In the East, as in the West, the 'heavenly' three-point symbol is in widespread use, in the most ancient as well as in modern civilizations, as a spiritual graphic with multiple meanings—mostly religious or magical. Different religions throw up meanings such as: three gods/trinity (Father, Son and Holy Ghost/the Trimurti: Shiva—destruction; Brahma—creation; and Vishnu—preservation ...); the eye of God; and so on.

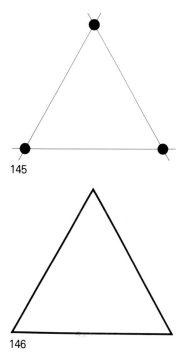

145

146

The three points often stand for: father (man), mother (woman), child.

The magical triangle is a device used frequently in the black arts: the exorcists' sign, or hallmark, for the devil. In Chinese writing, the triangle (△) is the union of three lines (= different things), and means: bring together, collect ... In the Cabbala, the letter ♥ (sh) means 'fire', 'the Trinity in God', and makes the tetragrammaton end in Yoshua. The descending dove stands for *shin*, while the three points on the wings and tail symbolize the three points of fire (Luke 3:22 and Matthew 3:16–17). Servius has the three points signifying birth, life and death. In a late-Christian sense, the three-point motif can be the symbol for faith, hope and charity.

Freemasonry too uses three points in its symbolism: beauty, power and wisdom (the three pillars); past, present, future/birth, life, death/light (active), darkness (passive), time (equilibrium: man–woman); and the triangle-with-the-eye (147). Sometimes the brothers tattoo the three points onto the hand, or elsewhere upon the body, and put it after (or in)

147

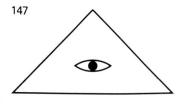

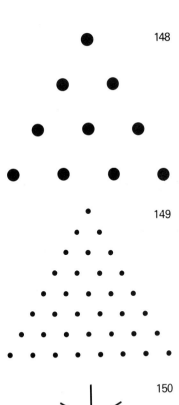

148

149

150

151

their signature. The masonic symbol, a pair of compasses, also refers to the three points. There is also, in masonic symbolism, the cosmic triada or radiating delta, whose sides mean: duration, darkness and light.

In numerical mysticism (the trigonal numbers) of the Cabbala and freemasonry, the number 3—and therefore also the three points—is especially significant, and is derived from Pythagorean systems.

Thus, for example, the first *tetraktys*: $1 + 2 + 3 + 4 = 10$ (148). The second *tetraktys* gives the sum: $5 + 6 + 7 + 8 = 26$ $(10 + 26 = 36)$. Now $36 = 6^2$—but it is also the triangular number of 8, or the sum of the addition of the first eight figures, the result of which is the graphic next to this (149).

Among African hunting tribes, three points can refer to hunter, dog and game.

In present-day Western 'tattoo language', the three-point sign can be the symbol of faith, hope and charity. In criminal circles, three points may be tattooed in the V between the thumb and index finger, enabling the sign to be concealed when in contact with the police or a court of justice simply by closing the fingers. Mostly the meaning is simple: 'criminal'. Sometimes there is an extra nuance: *mort aux vaches!* (down with the cops!) in France, or, in Germany, homosexual, work-shy and addicted. Many ex-prisoners have it tattooed conspicuously so as to make quite plain to society that they have been in prison and they carry this sign as a mark of mutual recognition.

In Italy, five tattooed points are a code used in criminal and Mafia environments, with a type of cross formed out of the middle, central point (150), the whole thing meaning: 'criminal'. One point stands for faith, one for hope, one for enclosed and one for freedom. The cross means: 'the prison'. This can perhaps be related to the *quincunx* (page 103), originally an ancient Roman coin weighing 5 ounces, from which many diamond-shaped and square structures that have a fifth point as a centre (151) may be derived.

Then there is the triangle itself, in particular the equilateral one, either pointing upwards (152, a.), or downwards (152, b.); it is used extensively in magical or religious contexts: for example, the magical triangle/the nimbus. The two opposing triangles placed on top of each other (or halved diamond) (153, a.) are a reflection of the mountain (the super-natural) and the cave (the subterranean, the chthonic centre of the earth)—again, an opposed but complementary jux-taposition. When this figure is rotated, it becomes a vulva symbol (153, b.). (See also mandorla, page 96.)

153

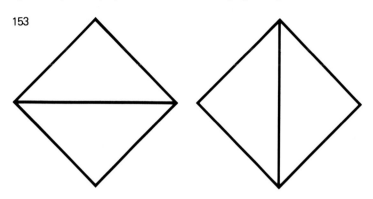

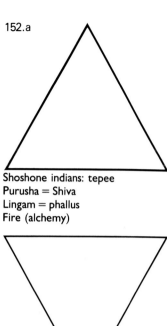

152.a

Shoshone indians: tepee
Purusha = Shiva
Lingam = phallus
Fire (alchemy)

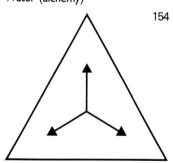

152.b

Prakriti = Shakti
Yoni = vulva
Water (alchemy)

In the alchemists' triangle, one point stands for salt, the second for sulphur, and the third for mercury.

Dynamically, the triangle is powerfully eccentric, with a strong motion outwards from an imaginary centre towards three acute corners; it is the most dynamic and aggressive of the basic forms (154). Its possible origin can be seen equally in a diagonal crossing + horizontal (and vertical) structure (155), or in a horizontal–vertical structure crossed by diagonals (156). But it may very well be that it comes about by simply connecting three points, a sort of graphical (*gestalt*) comple-tion (145). A step further, the right-angled triangle could have resulted from halving or quartering the square (157, a.b.). And a further possibility is that the triangle originates from

154

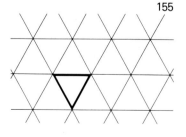

156a. Canary Islands   b.

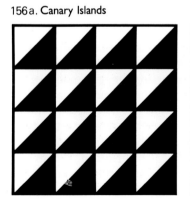

155

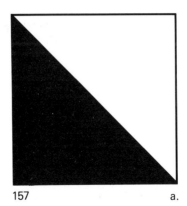

157   a.   b.

the combination of a horizontal and a wedge ($\wedge + \underline{} = \triangle$, or $\vee + \overline{} = \triangledown$).

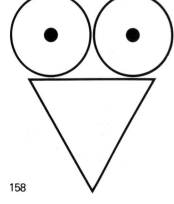

158

The V-shaped wedge can have a sexual interpretation: the pubic triangle. The triangle is also the obvious connection between the three female sexual organs: the breasts and genitals. Probably primitive heart-symbolism carried a similar sexual connotation of the genitalia combined in a single triangular symbol—for the triangle ($\triangledown$) has always been the symbol of the heart, *triangle du cœur* (158). In Tantrism, the heart-symbol represents the union between man, or the masculine principle (*pronisha*), and woman, or the feminine principle (*prakriti*). And the face has the same triangular structure, in the eyes, nose and mouth, as the breasts, umbilicus and pubic hair of a woman—an observation Magritte focused on in his painting *The Rape*.

In the Korean *han'gul* script, the triangular wedge-shape, pointing upwards, is phonetically *s*. Originally this was an image for the incisors ($\wedge$).

Among the Dogons, the triangle, pointing downwards, is the fertilizing masculine principle.

In the Greek alphabet, the triangular letter delta has a matrix symbolism. It is also the basis of the Hellenistic architectural pediment. In the triangular pediment of a temple, Pythagoras claimed to see the threefold nature of man, and of the cosmos, microcosmos and macrocosmos, the whole crowned by the divine unity, which itself is a trinity.

The 'Holy tetrad, this immense and pure symbol, source of nature, and model of the gods' (the *Golden Poems* of Pythagoras) ... At one and the same time this is the key to the universe, and the science of numbers: the ternary law that governs man. Pythagoras supposed also that the heavenly bodies move in accordance with the harmony and rhythm of the holy numbers.

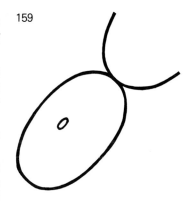

In any elementary symbolism—for example, among the North American Indians—the triangle, pointing upwards, can mean 'mountain', 'summit'; sometimes also 'tent' (tepee) or 'house' (tectiform).

The optimistic triangle, pointing upwards, is the Hittite hieroglyphic sign for 'life', or 'vital power'.

In the Greek alphabet, and thus also in other European alphabets, the triangular shape of the A is derived from the Phoenician ideogram (160), which was a stylized bull's-head (*alp* in Canaanite/*aleph* in Hebrew = bull). In the older proto-Sinaitic script, we find the same sign, a precursor of the triangular sign and with the characteristic bull's-head pattern (159). The formally drawn triangle, it may reasonably be supposed, is a schematization of the earlier hieroglyphic, pictographic sign.

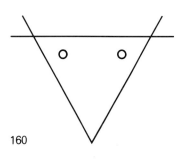

In Phoenician script, the basic form tilts to the right (161, 1.), and in ancient Greek, after still further fluctuation (161, 2.), it lands on its present base (161, 3.). The Roman A was a symmetric, balanced interpretation of the Greek A (161, 3.).

160

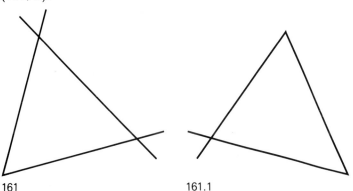

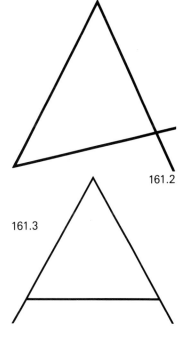

161   161.1   161.2

161.3

In cave drawings from the Palaeolithic Stone Age found in Lascaux, France, downwards-pointing triangular forms are seen to be vulva symbols, because of the vertical vulva-scratch (162). This vulva-symbolism is also found in the East, in Tantrism, for example, where the triangle, pointing downwards (152, b.)—the yoni, or Shakti—is feminine: the opposite of the masculine inversion (152, a.)—the Shiva. Sometimes the yoni is also made explicit with a vertical vulva-scratch (163).

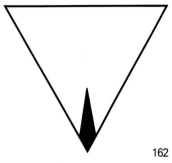

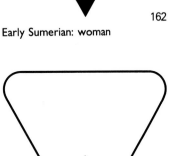

Early Sumerian: woman

162

163

Two or more inverted triangles, placed across each other and in their turn forming smaller triangles, produce the union of the masculine and feminine. The Tantric triangle, pointing downwards (yoni = vulva) has a dot (*bindu*) in the middle; the latter means 'the seed-sperm' (Shri Yantra) (164, 1.), and the whole is a fertility symbol. The triangle pointing upwards, with a dot, means 'the eye of God' (164, 2.).

Masculine and feminine triangles, drawn across each other, also produce the seal of Solomon, or *Magon David*—the Cabbalistic inversion:* 'as above, so below' (*quod superius sicut quod inferius*) (165). The symbolism of the seal, in alchemy, is represented in the drawing below (166, 167).

In the masonic Seal of Solomon, the triangle pointing upwards represents divinity, forces in development and spiritual fire (*kether* = the crown). Simultaneously opposite and complementary to this is the triangle pointing downwards, which represents earthly powers and man himself (*asiah* = matter).

Sengai calls the triangle the first tangible form, and the root of all other forms. The first form born of it is the square (= two triangles). And Plato maintained that the plane (flat surface) consists of triangles.

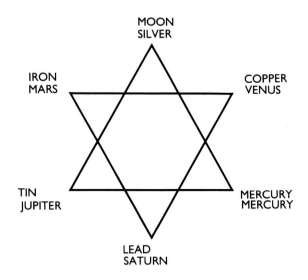

166

*In Cabbalistic symbolism: *teferet*, meaning 'truth and beauty'.

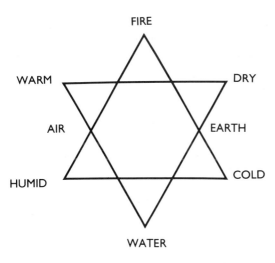

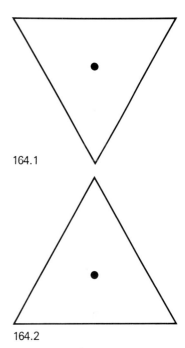

164.1

164.2

The fork (trident; in Hinduism: *trisula* = *wardhamana* = sickle of the moon) is a widely found ternary sign, apparently related to the triangle (168, a.b.). It consists of three elements: the double-wedge sign (\ + / = V), plus the bisection of the angle formed by the wedge. Possibly it originated from the androgynous, schematicized figure of man, with his arms stretched towards heaven; certainly it acquires that significance when the vertical line is pulled through the V (168, b.). This sign can be a symbol for 'king' and 'power' (for example, in proto-Indian script). In Tantrism it is a Shiva-sign—the *Om* sign. Whether pointing downwards or upwards, the sign can

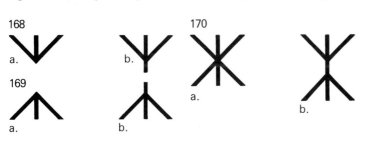

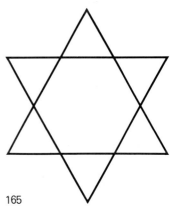

165

Magon David
Flemish house-mark
Hindu symbolism: shakra of the heart

acquire various symbolic meanings, but they can be paradoxical, and therefore confusing. For example, the fork, pointing downwards (168, a.b.), is the sign for: vulva, fertility, life, tree, growth. But equally it can mean: ruin, destruction, rejection, negation, instability. Pointing upwards, it means: phallus (either erect, or with the phallus hanging down between the outspread legs), arrow, root, androgynous sign ... vital and active, in other words. But other meanings include: shelter (runic sign), destruction, decay, dying. It can also be a tectiform, meaning: shelter, protection, house (169, a.b.).

The two signs can also be combined (170, a.b.). (See also the *chrism*.) There can be various double meanings, such as: tree (root-and-crown, in Chinese); the androgynous, schematized representation of man, again; or complementary facets, as are found in other yin-yang signs. When two symbols are combined around a common centre (170, a.), one of the astral signs, current in prehistoric times, is formed.

The old Chinese bone-writing pictogram for 'tree' (170, c.) is clearly related to the double wedge (170, b.). In Kai Ssu it became 170d.

The triangle has received scant attention in 20th-century art. Seuphor founded the magazine *Cercle et Carré*, but ignored the triangle. Artists such as Herbin, Vasarely, Klee, Kandinsky, Kupka and Vordenberge-Gildewart did use it quite frequently, but, as a rule, the triangle occurs only rarely in the paintings of most artists working from a geometrical basis.

170.c

CHAPTER 4

MAN AND PRIMEVAL GEOMETRY

Jorge Donn in *Mass for Our Time*
by Maurice Béjart (Photo: A.
Béjart)

MAN
AND THE GEOMETRY
OF THE BODY

The geometry of the body has always held a certain fascination for man. Standing up, he is vertical (fig. 52). Lying down, he is horizontal. His face and whole body are binary and symmetrical. His eyes, ears, shoulders, arms, hands, feet, breasts and testicles come in pairs. He uses his body, or parts of his body, as basic units of measurement—talking of the length of a thumb, the span of a hand, the width of a finger (or fingers); the foot, yard or step; the thickness of a fist; the height of a man; and so on.

As early as the 1st century B.C., Vitruvius made a study of the proportions of the human body. He found that the face, measured from the chin to the hairline, is one-tenth the length of its owner's body. So too is the distance from the wrist to the top of the index finger. From the middle of the chest to the crown of the head is one-quarter of the body's length, and from the chin to the crown of the head is one-eighth of that length. From the chin to the base of the nose is one-third the length of the face, and is equal to the distance from the base of the nose to the bridge of the nose, and from the bridge of the nose to the hairline. The foot is one-sixth the length of the body, and the forearm a quarter of its length. At the centre is the navel (fig. 53).

Hildegarde von Bingen, abbess of Rupertsberg in the 12th century, proposed that man, either in body length or across the span of his arms, can be divided into five equal lengths; that he has five senses; that there are five elements connected to the trunk (two arms, two legs and a head); and that for these reasons the pentagram is a sign of the microcosmos, reflected in the hand-and-five-fingers.

The Cabbalist, Agrippa von Nettesheim (1486–1536), also explored the relationship between man and the pentagram. The Cabbala gives 9 (3 × 3) as the standard human measure (fig. 54).

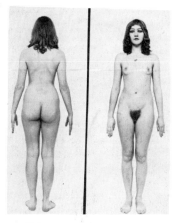

Fig 52
Illustration from *This Is Not A Book* by Mark Verstockt.

Fig 53
Drawing made in 1684, based on the principles of Vitruvius. The three scales on the right represent the ideal human proportions, according to the Greeks, the Romans and the French.

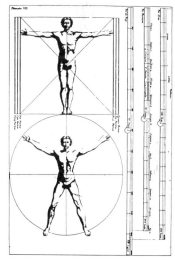

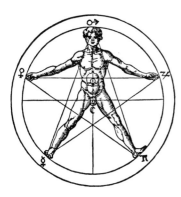

Moving on from Vitruvius, Leonardo established the geometric relationship between the square and circle, and the geometrical proportions of the human body (fig. 56). Dürer, influenced by Leonardo and Alberti, wrote on the same subject in his *Vier Bücher von Menschlicher Proportion* (fig. 55), a work published posthumously by Prikheimer in 1528, because Dürer, during his lifetime, altered it too often and therefore never considered it to be really fit for publication.

In African primitive sculpture, there are geometric—even cubist—structures. The stylized, geometrically schematized human form is found universally, as, for example, in archaic sculptures from the Greek Cyclades islands. Body-paintings of primitive warriors highlight the main features and elements of the human body, often resulting in geometric forms.

In adorning the body an order is superimposed on an existing order, respecting or sometimes contradicting the symmetries of the organic form. Gombrich—*The Sense of Order*.

Swiftly drawn graffiti and fluently drawn ideograms of the human body are geometrical.

More familiar are the Bauhaus drawings of Schlemmer (fig. 58), Le Corbusier's *Modulor* and Dreyfuss' *The Measure of Men*—and, of course, the schematized paintings of the Cubists and the Russian Suprematists.

Fig 54
This vision of Cosmic Man by the Cabbalist Agrippa von Nettesheim places man in the middle of a circle. A five-pointed star links head, hands and feet at the points of the star. The horizontal and vertical diameters of the circle intersect at his genitals.

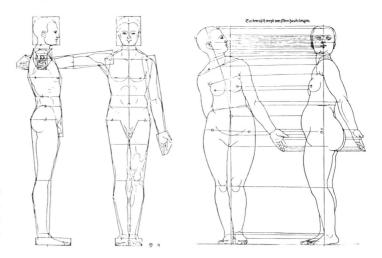

Fig 55
In his *Vier Bücher von Menschlicher Proportion*, Albrecht Dürer investigated the relations between the proportions of the human body and geometry.

Pursuing this line of thought, we also find geometry in everyday human behaviour. We walk in a straight line from one point to another. If we throw a spear, it flies in an arc, or bow. A lasso is swung with a circular motion. Our legs spread apart to form a triangle; our arms and legs, extended, form a cross. A round-dance describes a circle; other dances are based around parallel rows of partners; Zuni Indians and Dervishes whirl in spirals. People stand in parallel next to each other (fig. 59). Angles are formed when an arm or leg is articulated; roads join or cross to form angles. Add to this man's consciousness of rhythm in his own body—the pulsing of the heart, the rhythm of walking, stepping, strolling, breathing, eye-blinking, mating, hammering, chopping—and the origins of rhythm in man's creativity are easily seen.

One step further still, looking now at man's collective behaviour, the basic forms of the dwelling-place, temple and meeting-hall clearly evolved from geometrically-based functionalist forms: the circle, square and triangle. Next, on a larger scale, emerged the geometry of the market square, public forum, place of ritual (fig. 60), theatre (fig. 61), sporting arena, circus, courtroom, and army camp. Finally, the largest collective forms evolved: whole communities, villages and towns: circular, concentric, square, chequerboard-style, star-shaped: Stonehenge (fig. 62), the Breton dolmens, the Celtic megalithic lines, the Gallic cromlechs, the observatory at Jaipur, burial places, market squares, the Cherokee-Indian 'rotundas'... Everywhere, the primary drive is to create a structure that conforms to a clear geometric pattern—in major public spaces most of all.

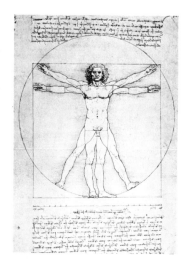

Fig 56
Leonardo da Vinci

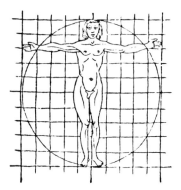

Fig 57
Geofroy Tory

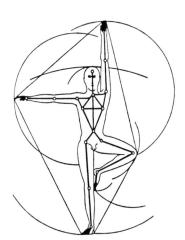

Fig 58
In the fourth publication of the *Bauhaus Bücher* (*Die Bühne im Bauhaus*), Oscar Schlemmer showed this graphic of human dance movements. Taken from *The Bauhaus*, by Hans M. Wingler, The MIT Press, Cambridge, Mass. and London.

Fig 60
Folk festival, Morocco.
A circle forms around a central event. This is a wedding ceremony but there could just as well have been a story-teller, a medicine-man, musicians or dancers in the centre. Such naturally formed circles are also reflected in the shapes of ancient theatres, such as Epidaurus, sanctuaries, market places...

Fig 61
Epidaurus

Herodotus has provided us with a detailed description of the ancient Persian town of Ecbatana, built in 715 B.C. In the middle of the town stood the king's palace and treasure chamber. These were enclosed within high walls, brilliantly gilded. Around them, six concentric ramparts were raised, decorated with painted notches of many different colours: silver, orange, blue, fiery red, black and white. Outside these protective walls, the plebeians were permitted to live.

From the Greek Plutarch (Romulus, 12) comes a beautiful legend about the origins of the city of Rome. Romulus is supposed to have dug a round hole (*fossa = mundus*), into

118

which (as religious prescription required) the fruits of the earth were to be thrown as a symbolic offering. Around this he drew a large trench, using a plough pulled by a bull and a cow, to mark the borders of the future city; these were broken only by four gateways.

Traditionally, however, Rome is also known as *Urbs quadrata*, referring perhaps to the division of the city into four parts, with what Plutarch calls the *mundus* (cosmos) at the point where the horizontal and vertical lines intersect. This could alternatively be explained by the fact that antiquity—and certainly the Ancient Greek world—was obsessed by a form of squaring the circle. Plutarch alludes to this, claiming that Rome was at one and the same time circular (Arabic: *traba's*) and square (Arabic: *istadara*) in shape (171).

Fig 59
Parallelism

The circle–square concept is a kind of projection of humanity's vision of the cosmos, whereby man's *ego* is viewed in relation to the idea of the *higher*. It reflects a primitive drive to order the physical world according to a spatial archetype that has its roots in man's relationship to the *higher*, which, he supposes, guides and influences all activity within any given space. According to many writers, this *cosmic* concept would underpin any functional concept of space—or could they, at times, coincide accidentally?

Perhaps, as the basic, symmetrical, cross-shaped layout of the early Christian cathedrals evolved—the elongated central nave and high-altar corresponding to the human head, the choir (*le chœur*) to the heart—we can see confirmed the notion that man has always designed his sanctuaries to reflect his own *microcosmic self*, which, in medieval times, was clearly mirrored in the body of the crucified Christ.

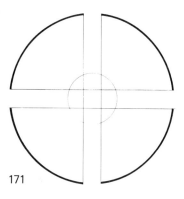

171

But the correspondence of the four points of the compass—the cross-shape—to the parts of the human body is not an exclusively Western, Christian phenomenon. It is found also among Red Indian tribes, such as the Yuroks of California. Lévi-Strauss calls this phenomenon:

La correspondance entre l'individuation géographique et l'individuation biologique: les êtres primitifs étaient informes, sans membres, et fondus ensemble, jusqu'à ce que survînt le Dieu Mangarkunjerkunja (le lézard-gobe-mouches) qui entreprit de les séparer et de les façonner individuellement.

Then there is the characteristic functional (defensive) plan of Roman *oppida* (towns), laid out in a grate, or chequerboard, form, and found all over Europe (172).

In Africa, Dogon cities are laid out on a concentric plan that finds an echo in the individual round-hut dwellings: the macrostructure reflected in the microstructure. Chinese villages are built to a uniform chequerboard plan, while the 17th-century city of Canton had a triangular plan, divided vertically and horizontally, chequerboard-fashion. Some Hopi villages also are of triangular design.

Arguably, when organizing and structuring flat or spatial forms, man resorts to geometry—even in its most basic, elementary form—because it ensures a methodical approach to controlling his designs. But also the very idea of geometry is implanted in man's body, providing a conscious or unconscious—but in either case reliable—framework of reference. Anthropomorphically-based geometry of this kind, revealing human creativity, providing the foundation for it, even, must rank as one of man's highest achievements. And that which evades geometry's controlling influence is sometimes called fantasy—but how often, in the event, is 'fantasy' merely uncontrolled chaos, a product of simple inability and ignorance?

Euclid's geometrical conquest of the basic forms was one of the culminating events in the process of humanizing our species. At last man could hold his ground in the midst of nature, using his intellectual faculties in a self-reliant, self-aware way. It marks a key stage in man's ordering and conquest of two- and three-dimensional space and of cosmic space itself.

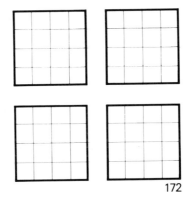

Fig 62
The architecture of Stonehenge demonstrates clearly the relation between the circle and time. It also illustrates the enclosure of a sacred place and the resultant isolation of this place from the space outside which is used for the activities of daily life: agriculture, hunting, housing... The enormous efforts prehistoric man made in order to build this monument—without leaving anything to chance—proves the importance he attached to the creation of this sanctuary.

172

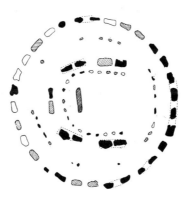

THE ALPHABET
AND GEOMETRY

Fig 65
Li-Ssu (Chinese seal writing)

Both the Greek (fig. 63) and Roman (fig. 64) alphabets are founded and structured on basic, elementary forms. I have restricted myself to these as examples because they are the most familiar; but an analogous structure could be demonstrated for the Chinese, Japanese, Korean, Arabic and Hebrew

Fig 63
Greek alphabet

alphabets; for the hieratic and demotic Egyptian scripts; and for most alphabetized pictographic forms of writing.

It is as if man himself, aware of the significance of his conquest of geometry, had channelled this awareness into semantic systems of communication. Or, further, that being once conscious of the semantic value of geometry, he had adapted his flowing scribbles to these functional, geometric forms—as in China during the Eastern Chin dynasty (317–420), where the famous calligraphers Wang Xizhi and Wang Xianzhi transformed the flowing *Li-Se* (also known as *Li-Ssu*, or *Li-Tzu*) script into characters based on the square (*Kai-Ssu* script) (fig. 65). In this way, Arabic writing acquired the Kufic form which, because of its legibility, is so readily applied in present-day advertising in Arabic countries (fig. 66).

Scientific studies of visual perception prove that geometri-

Fig 66
Kufic calligraphy: a labyrinth constructed on the name of Ali.

Fig 64
Roman alphabet

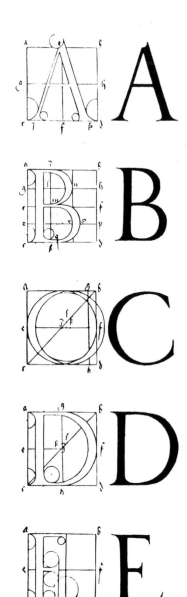

cally structured letter-characters are more practical and legible than flowing, calligraphic ones.

Fig 68
Geofroy Tory

Artists such as da Vinci (1505), Dürer (1525) (fig. 67) and Geoffroy Tory (1529) (fig. 68) all made geometric studies of the alphabet. Dürer especially, as an enthusiastic follower of Vitruvius' theory, thought it necessary and inevitable that geometry should be applied, not only in architecture, but also in the design of letters. The Renaissance writer Luca Paccioli (fig. 69) also studied the geometric structure of letters in his *De Divina Proportione* (1509). And later, to recall an

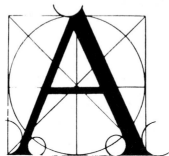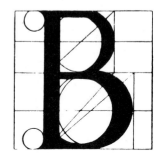

Fig 69   Luca Paccioli *De Divina Proportione*

example from our own century, at the Bauhaus, Herbert Bayer and Josef Albers used geometry as a starting point to structure their experimentation with letters.

Again and again, when modern man has sought to construct new systems of writing, or new signs, he has had recourse to geometry: in Braille, computer symbols, shorthand, signals of all kinds; and also in sign-systems invented by artists, as in the illustration of the work of A. R. Penck (fig. 70).

Fig 67
Albrecht Dürer
Unterweysung der Messung

Fig 70
The abstract, imaginary (?) signs of A. R. Penck are, like primary signs, based on geometry. This primitive sign (*Ohne Titel*, 1981) has a clear, underlying reference to a barbarian swastika; the arrows give dynamic support to the whole. (Photo: PVSK, Brussels).

Fig 70.1
Fragment of a Greek text carved in stone (Peloponnese, Greece). The geometric structures of the separate letters, and the visual impact of the letter O, combine remarkably to unify the image as a whole.

THE HUMAN SIGN

Fig 71
Man (Chinese).

Graffiti representing the human body, schematicized to a simple glyph, or groove, are to be seen on prehistoric cave-walls as much as on street walls in 20th-century cities. Their general clarity and legibility often depends on their precise cultural context, but for the social groups to whom they are addressed (and by whom they were drawn), they read quite explicitly regardless of how abstract or naturalistic their representation. The most abstract schematic rendering is the vertical line as a symbol for phallic, upright-standing man, with the 'head' dwelling in the cosmos—man representing himself

Fig 72

as the centre and pivot of the universe.

In the graffiti of certain cultures, there is a clear figurative distinction between the sexes. In others, man is represented as an asexual, androgynous figure.

Deep within man lies a primeval dread of visual representation of himself. (How many people—and not only among primi ive races—have a fear of being photographed?) Religions such as Islam and Judaism actually forbid visual representation of man.

There seem to be any number of hypotheses concerning the fact that prehistoric man represented animals naturalistically, but rendered man only in schematic form. Certainly this does not point to any technical inability to draw the human figure, for primitive artists will occasionally drop such elementary schematic styles when they wish, for example, to represent beings of a higher order.

Most remarkable of all, archetypal schematicizations of this kind can be found stereotyped everywhere as man's history unfolds. So, for example, the Chinese and Mayas used the same device as the inhabitants of the Steppes, the Red Indians or the cave-dwellers of the Mousterian; and so too do the present-day street-artists of New York or Paris.

I give here only a few glyphs, with no further reference—a random choice, out of hundreds of possible examples, that nevertheless indicates a kind of working evolution whereby the vertical, phallic symbol of man merges into the active, cosmic human figure (fig. 72).

Wall-painting by Bushmen (Southern Africa).

CHAPTER 5

TWENTIETH-CENTURY ARTISTS AND THE BASIC FORMS

YAACOV AGAM (France)
PIERRE ALECHINSKY (France)
AZUMA (Japan/Italy)
FRANK BADUR (Germany)
IGINO BALDERI (Italy)
VINCENT BATBEDAT (France)
MAX BILL (Switzerland)
MARI BOEYEN (Netherlands)
BRAM BOGART (Belgium)
WILLIAM BRAUHAUSER (Germany)
JOSÉ BREVAL (France)
NINO CALOS (France)
PAUL CITROEN (Netherlands)
CONTRERAS-BRUNET (France)
CORNEILLE (France)
GILBERT DECOCK (Belgium)
AD. DE KEYZER (Netherlands)
JO DELAHAUT (Belgium)
DEMARCO (France)
BRUNO DEMATIO (England)
DOMELA (France)
HUGO DUCHATEAU (Belgium)
DUSAN DZAMONJA (Yugoslavia)
XAVIER ESSELINCK (France)
MICHAEL FRIEDLÄNDER (Germany)
PAOLO GHILARDI (Italy)
HERMANN GOEPFERT (Germany)
ULLA GRIGUT-TROVE (Germany)
EVERT HILGEMANN (Germany)
GOTTFRIED HONNEGER (Switzerland)
OUTI IKKALA (Finland)
JOS JANS (Belgium)
PAAVO KAURAMÄKI (Finland)
WOLFGANG KLIEGE (Germany)

AXEL KNIPSCHIELD (Germany)
IMRE KOSCIS (Germany)
YVONNE KRACHT (Netherlands)
MATTI KUJASALO (Finland)
F. KYNCL (Germany)
WIFREDO LAM (Chile)
WALTER LEBLANC (Belgium)
HEINZ MACK (Germany)
BRUNO MUNARI (Italy)
M. NEMECZEK (Germany)
AURÉLIE NEMOURS (France)
JO NIEMEYER (Germany)
PAUL OSIPOW (Finland)
ROGER RAVEEL (Belgium)
RICARDON (France)
TORSTEN RIDELL (Sweden)
PETER ROYEN (Germany)
ALBERT RUBENS (Belgium)
RUSSEL SCARPULLA (U.S.A.)
H.D. SCHRADER (Germany)
MICHEL SEUPHOR (France)
SIAU-TSJIN (China/Italy)
DOM. STROOBANT (Belgium)
EMILIO TADINI (Italy)
TALEVA (Finland)
HEINZ TE LAAKE (Germany)
JOE TILSON (England)
WOODY VANAMEN (Netherlands)
GUY VANDENBRANDEN (Belgium)
DAN VANSEVEREN (Belgium)
JEF VERHEYEN (France)
MARK VERSTOCKT (Belgium)
LUDWIG WILDING (Germany)
ALBERTO ZILOCCHI (Italy)

ARTISTS
AND THE BASIC FORMS

I asked a hundred artists from all over the world to draw the three basic forms, with a view to making an effective image, or to indicate how they apply the forms in their own work. The contributions were striking in their variety, and the contrasts quite fascinating. My intention had been to demonstrate that there is no difference between, on the one hand, prehistoric, or primitive, examples and, on the other, the most up-to-date work; and also that each artist, while starting from the same basic idea, would develop nevertheless a personal interpretation of these forms. For each of them the abstract task was identical, but the results differed immensely.

The remarkable aspect was that while each drawing was usually done in the graphic style typical of its artist, it still retained certain generic characteristics. Thus the Orientals still remained Oriental, and the Constructivist artists were indeed more at home with the problems they confronted.

Strangely, quite a few artists were quite well able to handle either one or two forms, but had no idea what they would have done with more. A few seemed mystified. Others again had several ideas.

The drawings have not been arranged alphabetically, but have been printed unmodified and as received.

There is only one circle
There is only one square
There is only one triangle
There is only one system

There is no system
There is no triangle
There is no square
There is no circle

There are thousands of circles
There are thousands of squares
There are thousands of triangles
There are thousands of systems

There is

Ad de Keijzer

AD. DE KEYZER (Netherlands)

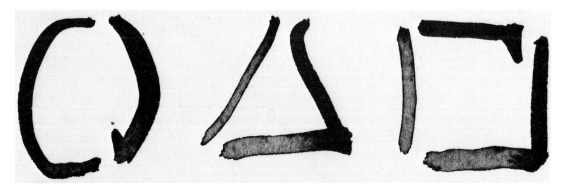

PIERRE ALECHINSKY (France)

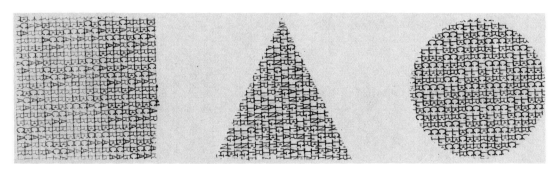

ALBERTO ZILOCCHI (Italy)

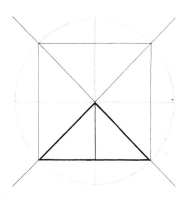

F. KYNCL (Germany)

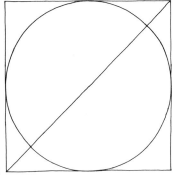

FRANK BADUR (Germany)

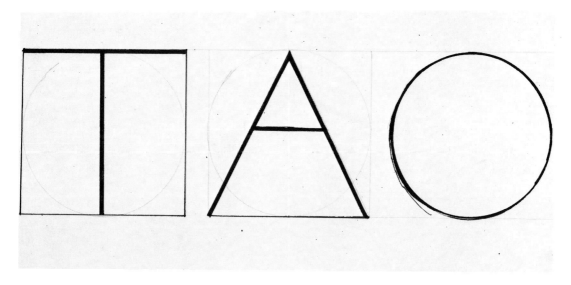

BRUNO DEMATIO (England)

WALTER LEBLANC (Belgium)

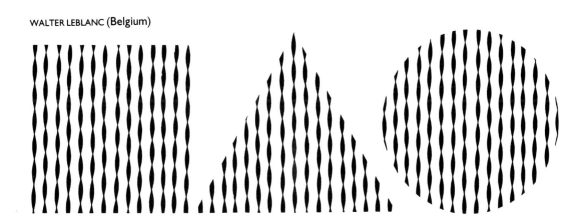

DEMARCO (France)

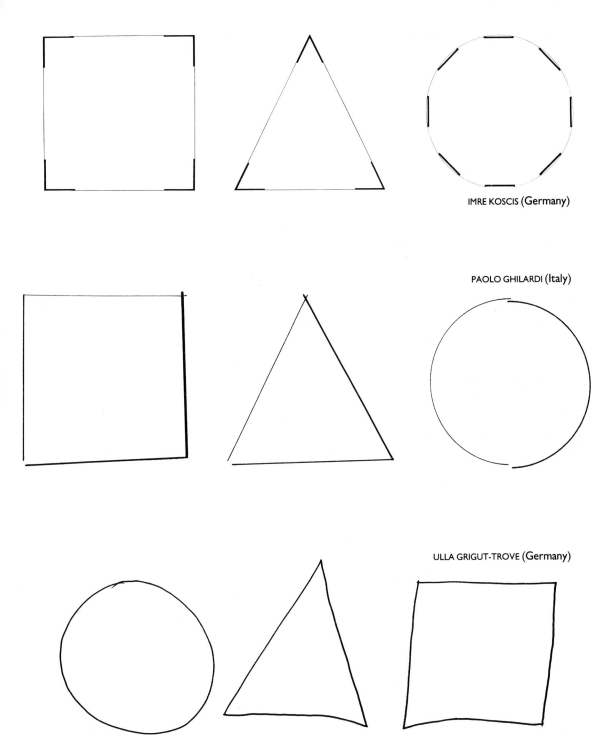

IMRE KOSCIS (Germany)

PAOLO GHILARDI (Italy)

ULLA GRIGUT-TROVE (Germany)

135

H.D. SCHRADER (Germany)

136

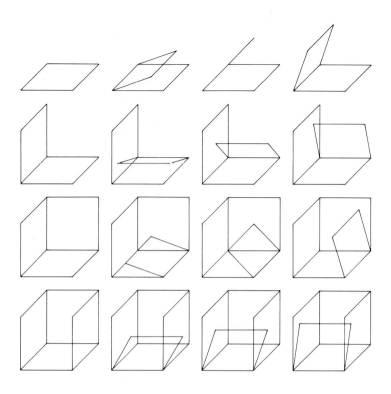

ALBERT RUBENS (Belgium)

GUY VANDENBRANDEN (Belgium)

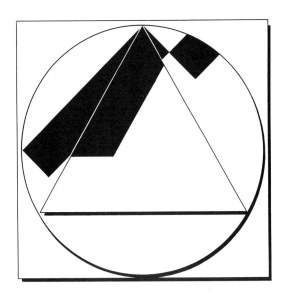

HEINZ TE LAAKE (Germany)

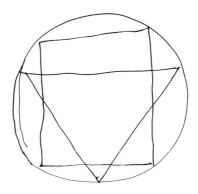

TORSTEN RIDELL (Sweden)

BRUNO MUNARI (Italy)

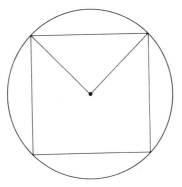

PAUL CITROEN (Netherlands)

AZUMA (Japan/Italy)

140

SIAU-TSJIN (China/Italy)

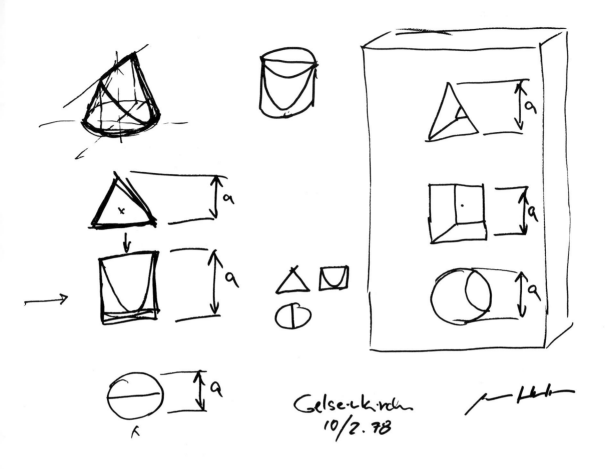

Gelsenkirchen
10/2.78

MICHAEL FRIEDLÄNDER (Germany)

JEF VERHEYEN (France)

$$\frac{A}{B} \ \text{blijft} \ \frac{B}{C}$$

$$\frac{A}{B} = \frac{B}{C}$$

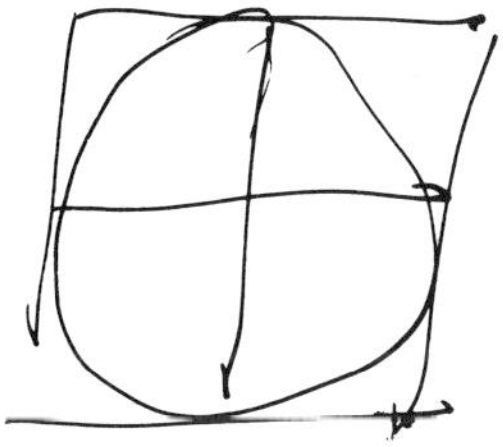

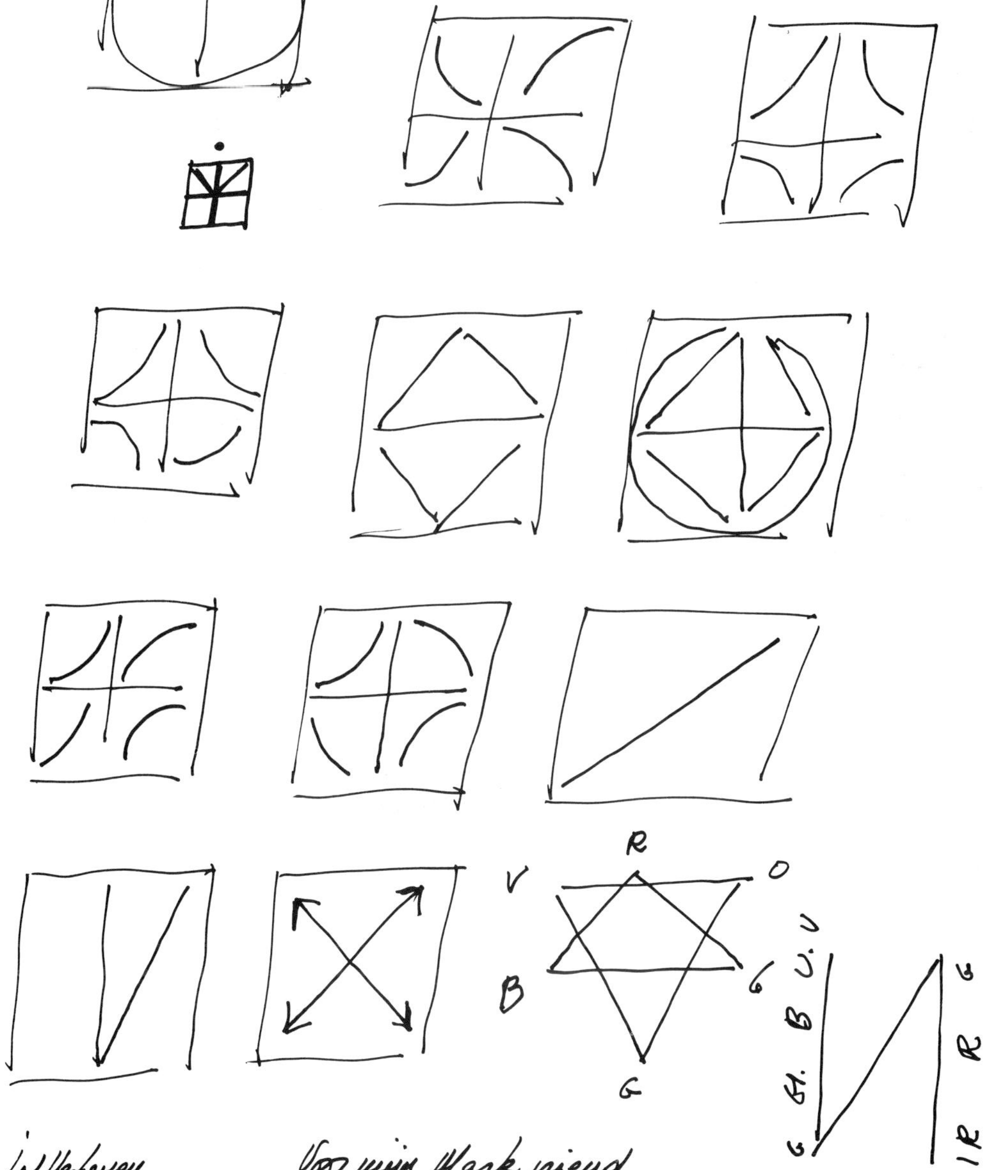

R   O

V

B

G

R. B. U. V

G   R   G   IR

Jef Verheyen

Peintre Flamand †

Voor mijn Mark vriend

Antwerpen 1950 - 2000 + $\frac{A}{B} = \frac{B}{C}$

143

JOS JANS (Belgium)

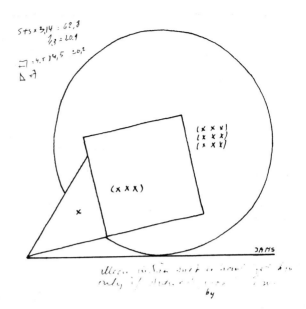

WIFREDO LAM (Chile)

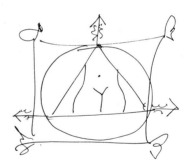

WOODY VANAMEN (Netherlands)

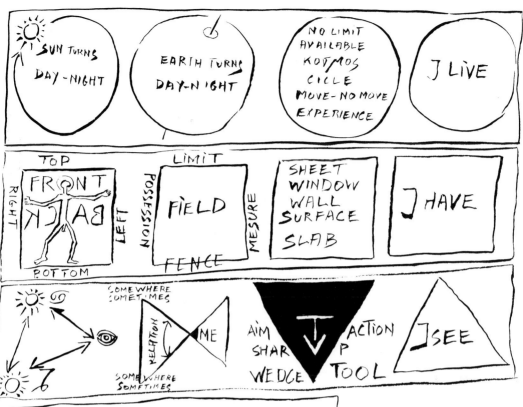
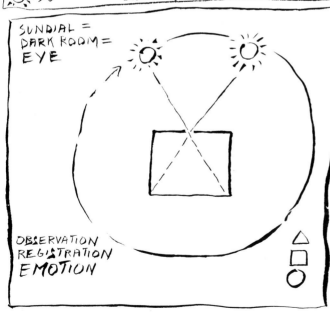

24 MAG. 1979

DOM. STROOBANT (Belgium)

Zo heb ik van de cirkel
de ronde bocht gebruikt
om de ruimte in te gaan.

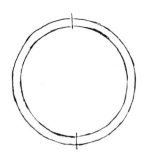

van de driehoek
de scherpe hoek

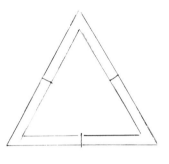

van het vierkant
de rechte hoek:

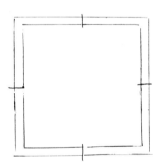

YVONNE KRACHT (Netherlands)

AURÉLIE NEMOURS (France)

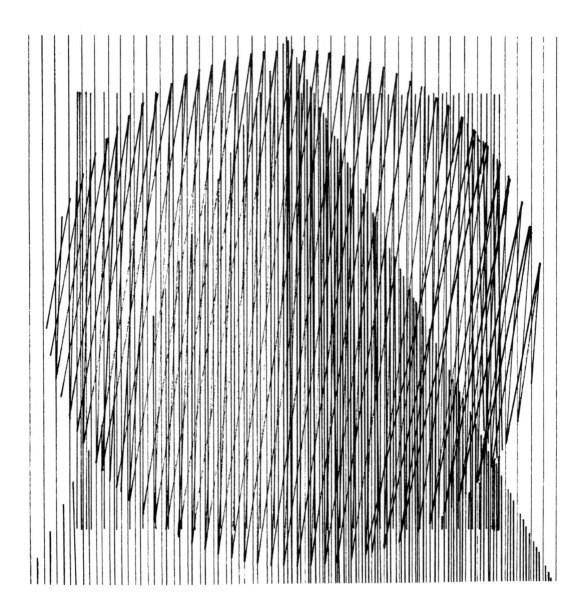

NINO CALOS (France)

148

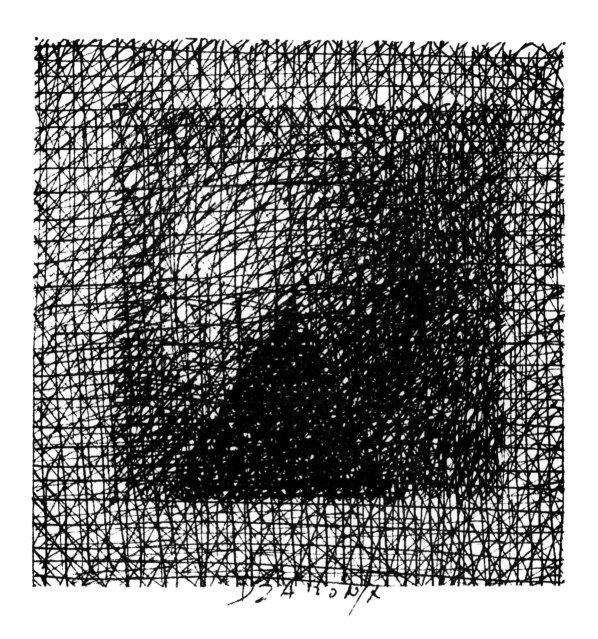

DUSAN DZAMONJA (Yugoslavia)

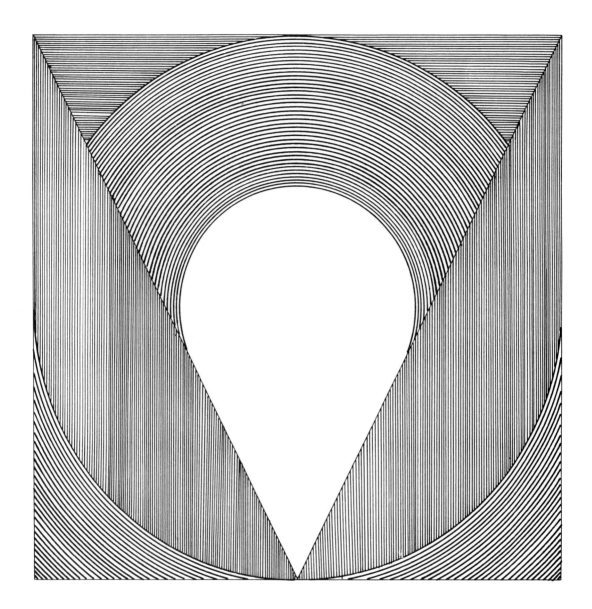

RUSSEL SCARPULLA (U.S.A.)

150

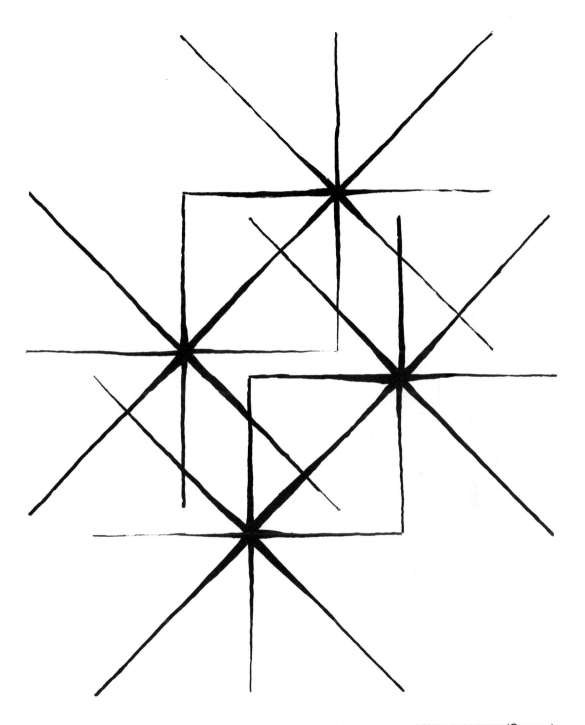

HERMANN GOEPFERT (Germany)

EMILIO TADINI (Italy)   CONTRERAS-BRUNET (France)

VINCENT BATBEDAT (France)

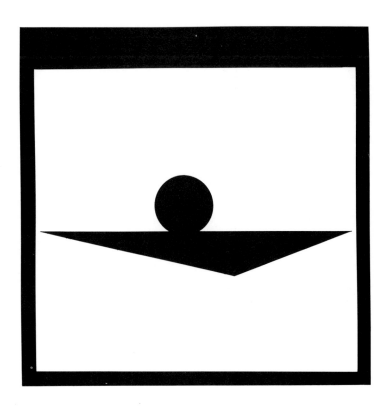

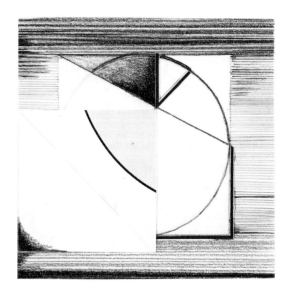

PETER ROYEN (Germany)

154

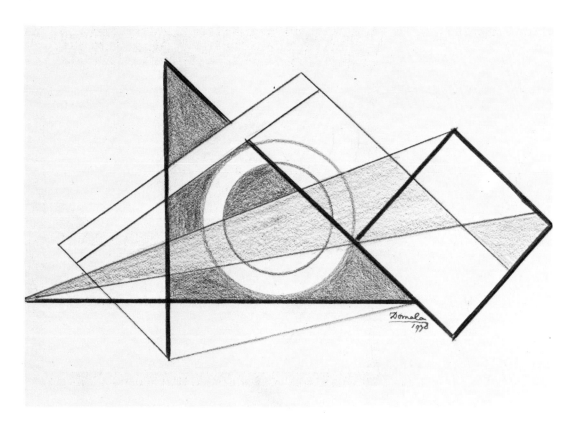

DOMELA (France)

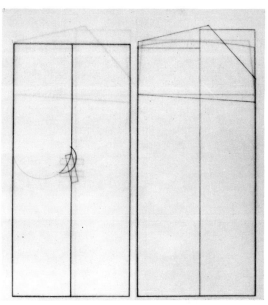

WOLFGANG KLIEGE (Germany)

155

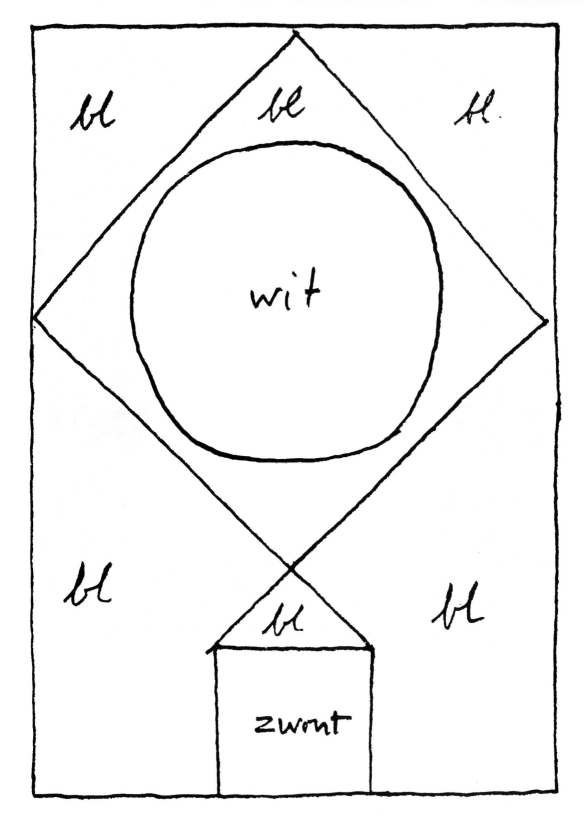

DAN VANSEVEREN (Belgium)

BRAM BOGART (Belgium)

157

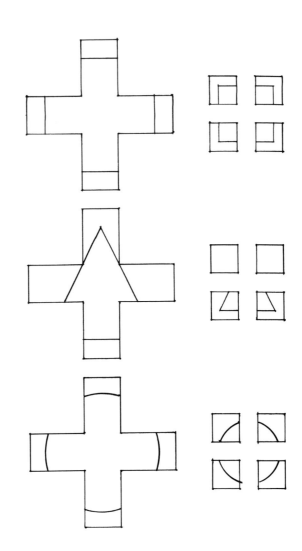

PAUL OSIPOW (Finland)

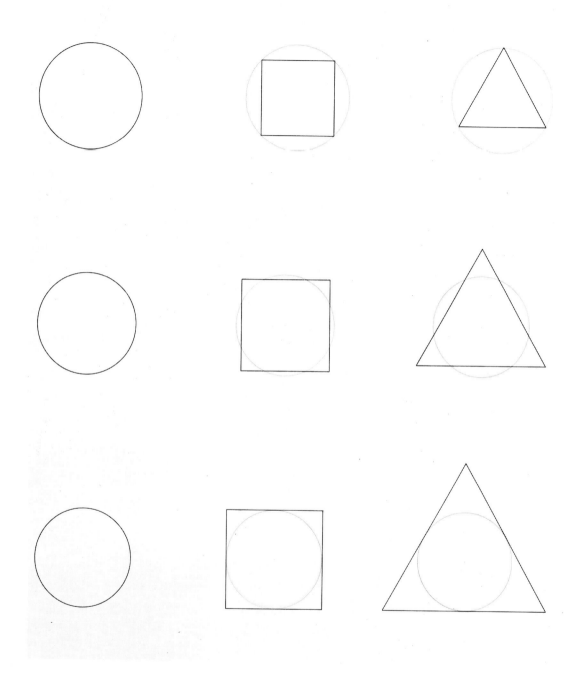

JOSÉ BREVAL (France)

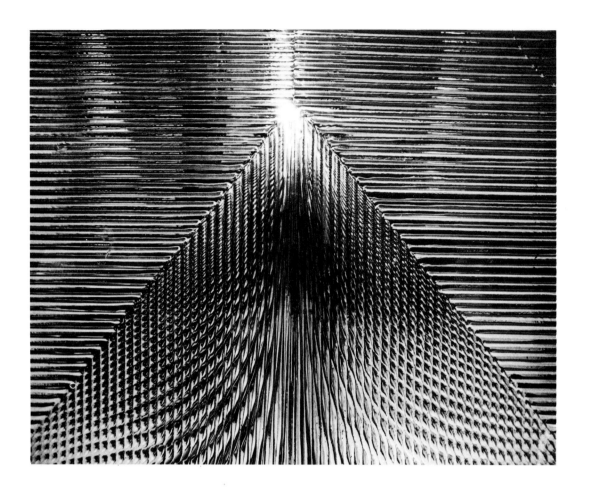

HEINZ MACK (Germany)

160

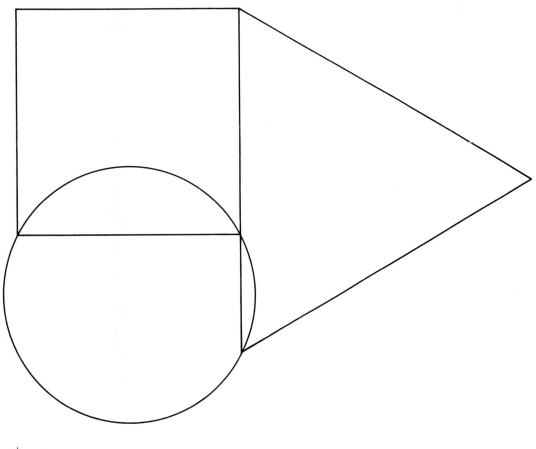

bill
1979

konglomerat von drei formen gleichen flächeninhalts

MAX BILL (Switzerland)

JOE TILSON (England)

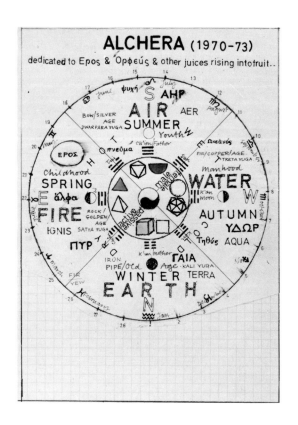

MARK VERSTOCKT (Belgium)

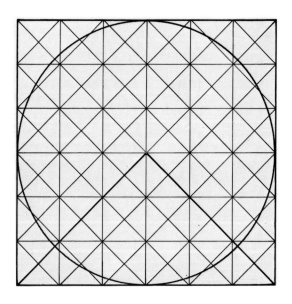

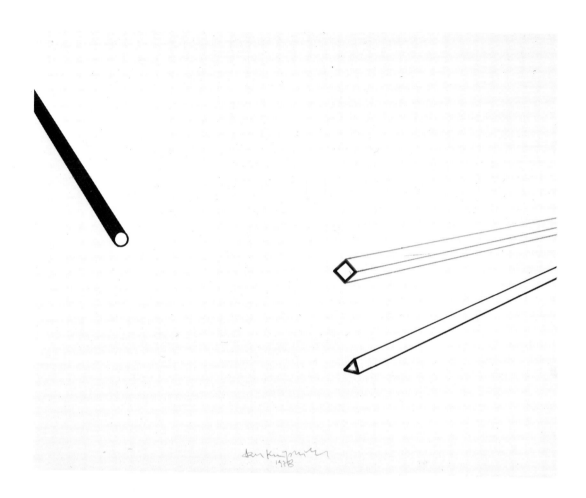

AXEL KNIPSCHIELD (Germany)

163

GILBERT DECOCK (Belgium)

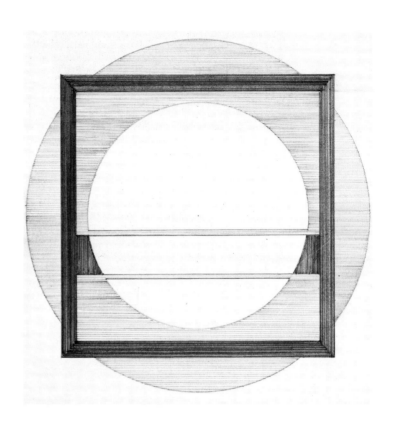

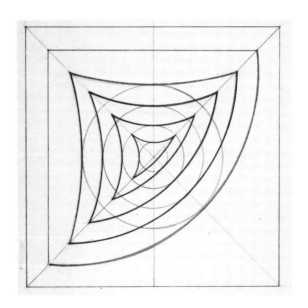

OUTI IKKALA (Finland)

164

JO NIEMEYER (Germany)

TALEVA (Finland)

165

HUGO DUCHATEAU (Belgium)

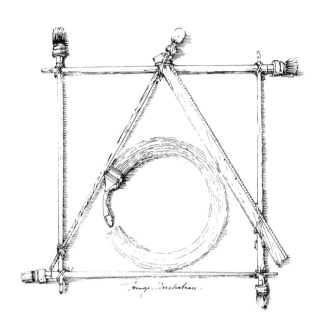

EVERT HILGEMANN (Germany)

ROGER RAVEEL (Belgium)

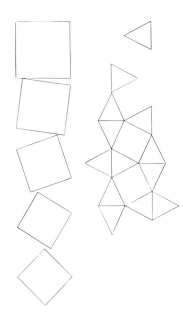

MATTI KUJASALO (Finland)

KONVERGENZ – STEREOSKOPIE

oder stereoskopisches sehen durch einen spalt (spalt-stereoskopie)

zeichnung a), b) und c) stellen paare dar, die sich stereoskopisch ergänzen. damit sie ihre räumliche wirkung entfalten können, müssen sie dem zuständigen auge getrennt dargeboten werden.

wenn man folgende anweisung genau beachtet, kann man mit ganz einfachen mitteln räumlich-stereoskopische wirkungen hervorrufen:
1. normale sitzhaltung am tisch (augenhöhe ca. 40 cm über tischkante).
2. zeichnung liegt auf dem tisch, die untere kante des blattes ca. 12 cm parallel zur tischkante.
3. hände mit handfläche nach oben ca. 20 cm über die zeichnung halten und zwar so, dass ein ziemlich breiter spalt (etwa 6-7cm) zwischen den beiden händen entsteht (genau symmetrisch zur zeichnung).
4. den spalt zwischen den händen solange gleichmässig verkleinern, bis die seitlichen linien des begrenzungs-quadrates für beide augen verschwinden. der spalt zwischen den handkanten sollte nun ca. 3 cm betragen.
   test: linkes auge schliessen, mit dem rechten auge darf man nur die linke zeichnung sehen. rechtes auge schliessen, mit dem linken auge darf man nur die rechte zeichnung sehen!
5. mit beiden augen sieht man jetzt nur noch *eine* stereoskopische figur, welche eine genaue räumliche position einnimmt.
6. die obere und die untere begrenzungslinie dient der kontrolle der parallelität von augenpaar zur zeichnungsachse. solange man noch sowohl oben als auch unten zwei parallele linien sieht, kann das stereoskopische sehen nicht funktionieren! durch leichte drehung des kopfes kann man die linien zur deckung bringen.
7. bei veränderung des augen-hand-abstandes verändert sich auch die räumliche position der stereoskopischen figur. dies kann soweit gehen, dass die zeichnung zwischen dem kopf und den handflächen zu schweben scheint, ein beweis für die komplexität unserer wahrnehmung.

seht oft gelingt das stereoskopische sehen nicht auf anhieb, hier hilft nur geduld und eigenes experimentieren. wer es aber einmal gesehen hat, ist überrascht und hat keinerlei probleme mehr.

mit diesem prinzip kann man auch gegenstandspaare stereoskopisch betrachten (z.b. zwei gleiche schnapsgläser oder zwei zigarettenpackungen). es ist erstaunlich, wie unsere räumliche wahrnehmung funktioniert und es bleibt der kreativität des betrachters überlassen, die schwerelosigkeit zu überwinden oder phantastische räumliche situationen zu erfinden.

hamburg 23-12-78   ludwig wilding

LUDWIG WILDING (Germany)

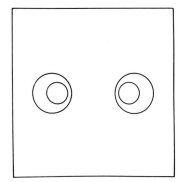
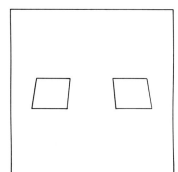
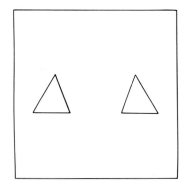

M. NEMECZEK (Germany)

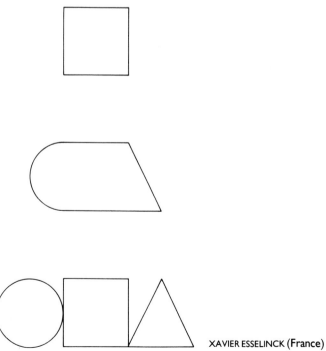

XAVIER ESSELINCK (France)

169

GOTTFRIED HONNEGER (Switzerland)

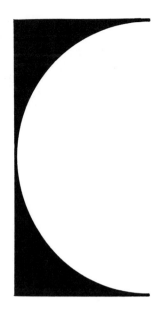

MICHEL SEUPHOR (France)

RICARDON (France)

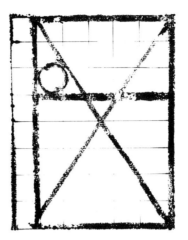 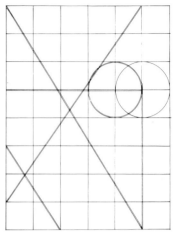

MARI BOEYEN (Netherlands)

172

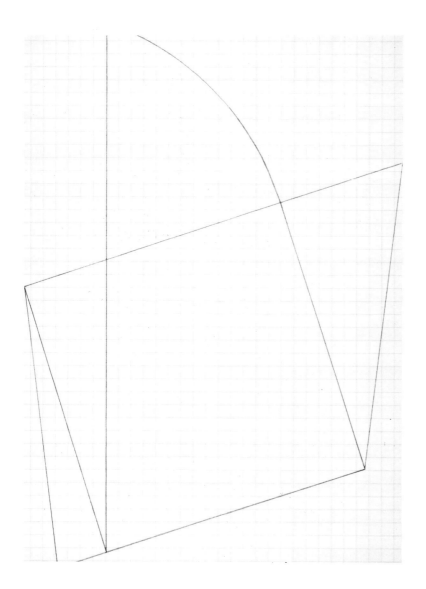

PAAVO KAURAMÄKI (Finland)

IGINO BALDERI (Italy)

174

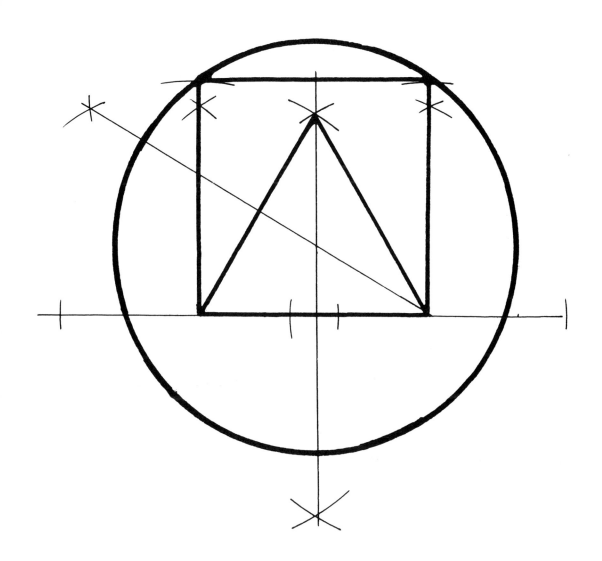

JO DELAHAUT (Belgium)

YAACOV AGAM (France)

CORNEILLE (France)

WILLIAM BRAUHAUSER (Germany)

178

BIBLIOGRAPHY

AGUIRE MANUEL —. LA ESCRITURA EN EL MONDO, Madrid, 1961

AICHER OTL — / KRAMPEN MARTIN —. ZEICHENSYSTEME DER VISUELLEN KOMMUNIKATION, Alex Koch GmbH, Stuttgart, 1977

ALBARIN KEITH — / MIAL SMITH JENNY —. DIAGRAM The Instrument of Thought, Thames and Hudson Ltd., London, 1977

ARNHEIM RUDOLF —. ENTROPY AND ART an Essay on Disorder an Order, University of California Press, Berkeley and Los Angeles, 1971
ART AND VISUAL PERCEPTION, University of California Press, 1954
ART AND VISUAL PERCEPTION; A Psychology of the Creative Eye. The new version, 1974

ASSOCIATION ARCHEOLOGIQUE KERGAL. Etudes et Travaux N° 2 – Juin 1977. N° 1 – Mai 1977

AZIZA MOHAMED —. LA CALIGRAPHIE ARABE, S.T.D., Tunis 1973

BACON EDMUND N. —. DESIGN OF CITIES, The Vicking Press, N.Y., 1967

BADER A. / SCHMIDT G. / STECK H. —. THOUGH THIS BE MADNESS, Thames and Hudson, London, 1961

BARBIER JEAN PAUL —. SYMBOLIQUE ET MOTIFS DU SUD DE NIAS, Etudes et monographies publiés par la collection BARBIER-MÜLLER, Genève, 1978

BIEGBEDER O. —. LEXIQUE DES SYMBOLES. Zodiaque, La Pierre qui Vire, 1969

BEDARD J.C. —. POUR UN ART SCHEMATIQUE: Etude d'un monoide graphique, Editions de Beaune & Editions Gontal-Darly, 1978

BIEDERMANN H. —. BILDSYMBOLE DER VORZEIT, Verlag der Sammler, Graz, 1977

BIERENS DE HAAN Dr J.D. —. UIT DE GESCHIEDENIS VAN DE METAPHISISCHE AESTETICA, Servire, Den Haag, 1943

BLOOMER CAROLYN M. —. PRINCIPLES OF VISUAL PERCEPTION, Van Norstrand Reinhold Company, N.Y.-Cincinati-Toronto-London-Melbourne, 1976

BOAS FRANZ —. PRIMITIVE ART, Dover Publications Inc, N.Y., 1955

BORD JANET —. MAZES AND LABYRINTHES OF THE WORLD, Latimer, London, 1976

BREFFNY BRIAN DE —. THE IRISH WORLD, London, 1977

BRIARD JACQUES —. L'AGE DE BRONZE EN EUROPE BARBARE, Ed. Des Hesperides, 1976

CAMPBELL GRANT —. THE ROCKPAINTINGS OF THE HUMASH, University of California Press, Berkeley and Los Angeles, 1976

CELLI GEORGIO —. ORIGINI DELL' ARTE, Galleria d' Arte Moderna, Bologna, 1975

CHAMPEAUX G. de —. / STERCKX, O.S.B. D. S. —. INTRODUCTION AU MONDE DES SYMBOLES, Zodiaque, Pierre Qui Vire, 1966

CHEVALIER J. / GHEERBRANT A. —. DICTIONNAIRE DES SYMBOLES, Rob. Laffont, Paris, 1969

CIRLOT J.E. —. A DICTIONARY OF SYMBOLS, Philosophical Library, Inc., N.Y., 1962

CLAUSBERG KARL —. KOSMISCHE VISIONEN, Mystische Weltbilder von Hildegarde von Bingen bis Heute, Dumont, Köln, 1980

COHEN MARCEL —. LA GRANDE INVENTION DE L' ECRITURE ET SON EVOLUTION, Imprimerie Nationale, Paris, 1958

COOPER J.C. —. TRADITIONAL SYMBOLS, Thames and Hudson, London, 1978
DOBLHOFER ERNST —. LE DÉCHIFREMENT DES ECRITURES, Arthaud, Paris, 1959
DONDIS A. —. A PRIMER OF VISUAL LITERACY, MIT, Massachusetts and London, 1973
DREYFUSS HENRY —. THE MEASURE OF MAN, Whitney Library of Design, N.Y..
    SYMBOL SOURCEBOOK, Foreword by BUCKMINSTER-FULLER, Mc Graw-Hill Book-company, N.Y., 1972
ECO UMBERTO —. SEGNO, Isedi, Milano, 1973
EHMER HERMANN K. —. VISUELLE KOMMUNIKATION Beiträge zur Bewustseins-industie, DuMont Aktuell-DuMont Schauberg, Köln, 1971
ELIADE MIRCEA —. IMAGES ET SYMBOLES, Ed. Gallimard, Paris, 1952
ELIADE MIRCEA —. LE SACRÉ ET LE PROFANE, Gallimard, Paris, 1965
GIEDION S. —. L'ETERNEL PRESENT, LA NAISSANCE DE L'ART (Franse versie) Ed. de la Connaissance s.a. – Brussel, 1965
GOBLET D'ALVIELLA, Graaf —. DE WERELDREIS DER SYMBOLEN (Herdruk – Fac-simile), W.N. Schors – Amsterdam
GUÉNON RENÉ —. SYMBOLES FONDAMENTAUX DE LA SCIENCE SACRÉE, N.R.F., Gallimard, Paris, 1962
    LE SYMBOLISME DE LA CROIX, L'anneau d'Or, Les Editions Vega, Paris, 1979
HADINGHAM EVAN —. CIRCLES AND STANDING STONES, William Heinemann, London, 1975
HALPRIN L. —. CREATIVE PROCESSES IN THE ENVIRONMENT, Georges Braziller Inc., N.Y., 1969
HARTWIG HELMUT —. SEHEN LERNEN, Kritik und Weiterarbeit am Kozept, DuMont Aktuell-DuMont Schauberg, Köln, 1976
HERITY MICHAEL —. IRISH PASSAGE GRAVES, Neolithic tomb-builders in Ire-land and Britain 2500 B.C., Harper and Row Publishers Inc., N.Y., 1975
HONEGGER A. —. FORMA E SEGNO; Romana Libri Alfabeto s.r.l., Roma, 1977
HUMBERT C. —. ORNAMENTAL DESIGN, Office du Livre, Fribourg, 1970
JACQ CHRISTIAN —. LA FRANC-MAÇONNERIE, Les Enigmes de l'univers, Lafont, Paris, 1975
JILL PURCE —. THE MYSTIC SPIRAL, Thames and Hudson, London, 1974
JUNG C. — / VON FRANZ H.L. — / HENDERSON J.L. — / JACOBS J. — / JAFFE A. —. MAN AND HIS SYMBOLS, Aldus Books Ltd., London, 1964
KANDINSKY WASSILY —. PUNKT UND LINIE ZU FLÄCHE, Bauhausbücher, 1926
KEESING F.M. —. CULTURAL ANTHROPOLOGY, Rinehart & Ciore, N.Y., 1958
KELLOG R. —. WHAT CHILDREN SCRABBLE AND WHY, San Francisco, 1955
KADATH —. Revue des civilisations disparues, Brussels. 1977.
KEPES GYORGY —. THE NEW LANDSCAPE in Art and Science, Paul Theobald and C°, Chicago, 1956
KLEIWEG DE ZWAAN Dr. J.P. —. PALEOLITISCHE KUNST IN EUROPA, H.J. Paris Amsterdam, 1930
KOENIG OTTO —. URMOTIV AUGE Neuentdeckte Grundzüge Menschlichen Verhaltens, Piper & C° Verlag, München-Zürich, 1975
KRISTEVA JULIA —.... LA TRAVERSÉE DES SIGNES, Tel Quel, Ed. du Seuil, Paris, 1975
KRIWET —. DIE WELT DER SCHRIFT- UND ZEICHENSPRACHE, Studio Dumont-DuMont-Schauberg Verlag, Köln, 1972
KUHN Prof. Dr H. -. AUF DEN SPURREN DES EISZEITMENSCHEN, Brockhaus, Wies-baden
LANG M. —. GRAFFITI IN THE ATHENIAN AGORA. American school of classical studies at Athens, Princeton, New Jersey, 1974
LANGER SUSANNE K. —. FEELING AND FORM, A theory of art develped form, Charles Scribner' Sons, N.Y., 1933
LEGEZA LASZLO —. TAO MAGIC, The secret language of diagrams and calli-graphy, Thames and Hudson, London, 1975
LEHNER E. —. SYMBOLS, SIGNS & SIGNETS, Dover Publications Inc., N.Y., 1969
LHOTE HENRI —. VERS D'AUTRES TASSILIS, Arthaud, Paris, 1976
LEPLAE CHARLES —. CHANT SUR LA RIVIÈRE, Essay sur la Poésie Chinoise, Les Editions des Artistes, Brussel.

LE ROY H. APPLETON —. AMERICAN INDIAN DESIGN AND DECORATION, Dover
   Publications Inc., N.Y., 1950-1971
LEROI-GOURHAN A. —. LE GESTE ET LA PAROLE, Technique et Langage. La
   Mémoire et les Rythmes, Albin Michel, Paris, 1964.
LEVI-STRAUSS CLAUDE —. LA PENSÉE SAUVAGE, Plon, Paris, 1962
MALLERY GARRICK —. PICTURE-WRITING OF THE AMERICAN INDIANS (1/2),
   Dover Publications, N.Y., 1976
MARC, OLIVIER —. PSYCHOLOGY OF THE HOUSE, Thames and Hudson, London
   1977
MENZEL BRIGITTE —. TEXTILIEN AUS WESTAFRIKA (1) (2) (3), Museum für Vol-
   kenkunde, Berlin 1972
MEREDIEU F. de —. LE DESSIN D'ENFANT, Psychothèque, Editions Universitai-
   res, Paris, 1974
MOOKERJEE A. — / KHANNA M. —. THE TANTRIC WAY. Thames and Hud-
   son, London, 1977
MUCHERY GEORGES —. LE TAROT DIVINATOIRE, Ed. du Chariot, Paris, 1965
MUNARI BRUNO —. ARTE COME MESTIERE, Laterza, Bari, 1966
   ARTISTA E DESIGNER, Laterza, Bari, 1978
   DISCOVERY OF THE SQUARE, Georges Wittenborn Inc., N.Y., 1965
   DISCOVERY OF THE CIRCLE, Georges Wittenborn Inc., N.Y., 1965
   LA SCOPERTA DEL TRIANGOLO, Zanichelli, Bologna, 1977
NATAF GEORGES —. SYMBOLES, SIGNES ET MARQUES, Berg International, édi-
   teurs, Paris, 1973
NAVEH JOSEPH —. ORIGINS OF THE ALPHABET, Cassel & C°, London, 1975
NELSON GEORGES —. HOW TO SEE. A Guide to Reading Our Manmade Envi-
   ronment, Little, Brown & C°, Boston-Toronto, 1977
PAPUS. TRAITE METHODIQUE DE MAGIE PRATIQUE. Ed. Dangles, Paris
PEDDE D. —. GEOMETRY AND LIBERAL ARTS, Pinguinbooks, 1976
PEIGNOT JERÔME —. DU CALIGRAMME, Dossiers Graphiques Du Chêne,
   Paris, 1978
PETRIE FLINDERS —. DECORATIVE PATTERNS OF THE ANCIENT WORLD FOR
   CRAFTSMEN, Dover Publications, N.Y., 1974
REUSCH J. — / KEES W. —. NON VERBAL COMMUNICATION, University of Cali-
   fornia Press, Berkely, Los Angeles, London
REVAULT JACQUES —. NORTH AFRICAN CARPETS AND TEXTILES, Dover Publi-
   cations, N.Y., 1973
RIDLEY M. —. THE MEGALITHIC ART OF THE MALTESE ISLANDS, The Dolphyn
   Press, 1971
ROUVRE EVRARD de —. PARURES AFRICAINES, texts of D. PAULME and J.
   HACHETTE, Paris, 1956
RUDOFSKY BERNARD —. THE UNFASHONABLE HUMAN BODY, Bupert Hart-
   Davis, London, 1972
   THE PRODIGIOUS BUILDERS, Martin Secker & Warburg Ltd., London, 1977
   ARCHITECTURE WITHOUT ARCHITECTS, Museum of Modern Art N.Y.
SCHMAND-BESSERAT D. —. THE EARLIEST PRECURSOR OF WRITING, Scientific
   American, June 1978, Vol. 238, Nr. 6
SCHURÉ EDOUARD —. LES GRANDS INITIES, Librairie Academique Perrin,
   Paris, 1960
SCHWARZ-WINKELHOFER I. / BIEDERMANN H. —. DAS BUCH DER ZEICHEN
   UND SYMBOLE, Knaur, München, 1975
SEUPHOR MICHEL —. LA TENDANCE A LA REPETITION DES SIGNES GEOMETRIQUES
   SIMPLES DANS L'ART CONTEMPORAIN. Niet uitgegeven
SHEETS DYE DANIEL —. CHINESE LATTICE DESIGN, Dover Publications Inc.,
   N.Y., 1974
SMEETS RENÉ —. ORNAMENT, SYMBOOL EN TEKEN, Cantecleer B.V., De Bilt,
   1973
STERN ARNO —. UNE GRAMMAIRE DE L'ART ENFANTIN, Delachaux et Niestle,
   1966
STEVENS PETER S. —. PATTERNS IN NATURE, Brown & Co, 1974
STOLPE HJALMAR —. AMAZON INDIAN DESIGNS, Dover Publications, N.Y.,
   1974

VERHOEVEN Dr. C.W. —. Symboliek van de voet, Van Gorcum, Assen, 1957
VERHOEVEN CORNELIUS —. Rondom de leegte, Ambo N.V., Utrecht, 1966
Het grote gebeuren, Ambo N.V., Utrecht, 1966
VERSTRAETE Dr. E. —. Huismerken en sibbeteekens in vlaanderen, uitg. Familia et Patria, 1979 (herdruk Fac Simile)
VOLLEMAERE A. —. Nouvelles interpretations de l'ecriture des codex mayas. Thèse de doctorat de 3e cycle, 1971
WALLIS BUDGE E.A. —. Amulets and Superstitions, Dover Publications Inc., N.Y., 1978
WERSIN WOLFGANG VON —. Das Elementare Ornament und Seine Gesetzlichkeit, eine Morphologie des Ornaments, Otto Maier, 1940, 1964

INDEX

SYNOPSIS: TABLE OF SIGNS AND FORMS

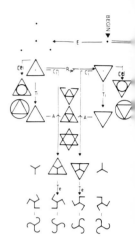

KEY

A = Basic element

E = Repetition of basic element

C = New element created by the joining of
     points (locked)

C_e = Closure of the outline (through locking
     of the elements)

C_i = Locking of the inner elements

R = Rotation

$R_{45°}$ = 45° Rotation

R_{∞} = 360° Rotation, full circle

Te = New element by omission of part (parts) of the outline
     (censorship)

Ti = New element by omission of inner part (parts)

— = Self evident progression

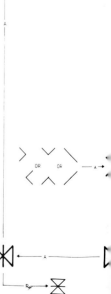

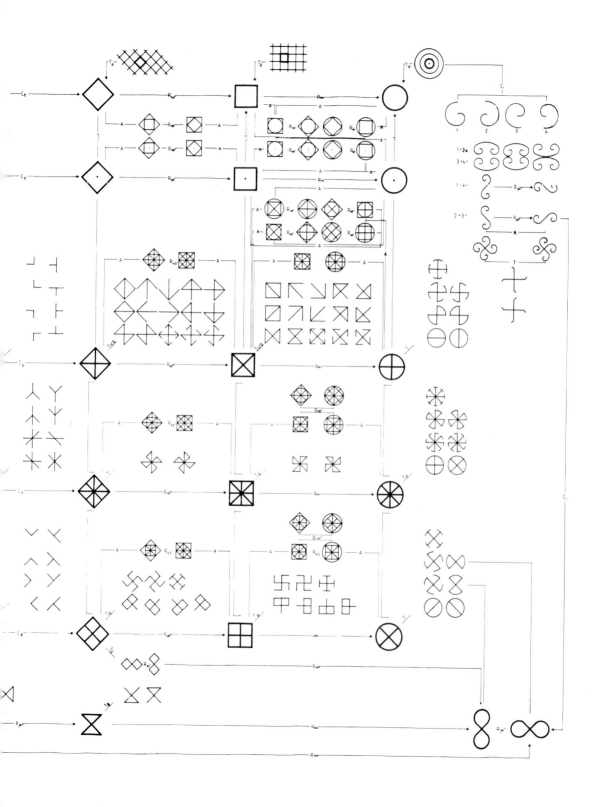

Photographs	RAOUL VAN DEN BOOM (B.)	B.-K. VERSTOCKT (B.)
	GERALD DAUPHIN (B.)	PHOTOGRAVURE DE SCHUTTER (B.)
	DRAG. KAZILIĆ (Y.)	LE ZODIAC (F.)
	GUY STEVENS (B.)	HANS SIBBELEE (H.)
	ALAIN BEJART (B.)	A. VAN DE GINSTE (B.)
	GALERIE BONIER (S.)	P.V.S.K.-BRUSSEL (B.)
	MUSÉE BARBIER-MÜLLER (S.)	PH. DE GOBERT (B.)
	A.C.L. (B.)	W. FORMAN ARCHIVES (GB.)
	CHRIS BOGAERTS (B.)	CIBA-GEIGY (S.)
	MUSEE D'ART MODERNE (B.)	THOMAS DAVID (A.)
Design	MARK VERSTOCKT	

Acknowledgements

The part my friends have played in the realization of this book is so great that the task of mentioning them all here is nothing but a dim reflexion of what I owe them.
Firstly, I have to thank GEORGES ADÉ, professor at the Catholic University at Louvain for his critical readings and re-readings of the book and for collaborating on the synoptic table of basic signs and forms. For their reading of the original manuscript, thanks to JO DUBOIS, LEO GEERTS and JEAN WARIE. I will never forget the many discussions and conversations with MICHEL SEUPHOR, BRUNO MUNARI, PHIL MERTENS, MARIA CLARA QUARENGHI, VERA HORVAT-PINTARIC, DAN VAN-MILETO, ERNST GOLDSCHMIDT, MARIA and ROBERT DELEVOY and so many others who helped me to gain an insight into such a complex subject. An accidental meeting with J.M. MORRISET in Rouan unleashed a stream of material for me to work with.
I have to thank LUENG SZE LEH, IKUO IKEDA and MISAO SHUKUNI for their help with the Chinese and Japanese ideograms.
Many thanks to all the artists, colleagues who collaborated to the very last. Also, I have to mention all the following who have acted as intermediaries between myself and the artists or have sent me useful material: Studio Marconi, Milan; Pa Szepan, Gelsenkirchen; Schoeller, Dusseldorf; Multi art points, Amsterdam; Bonier, Geneva; Museum Barbier-Müller, Geneva; Orez, The Hague; Numaga, Auvernier; S-65, Aalst; And last but not least, my thanks to my London publishers, Muller, Blond & White for their confidence and to Hal Robinson for his patient and enthusiastic help.

Translated from the Dutch by Pat and Andre Lefever